THE GOOD, THE BAD AND THE UGLY

MULLER

THE GOOD, THE BAD AND THE UGLY

Cities in Crisis

Rod Hackney
with Fay Sweet
Foreword by The Rt Hon
The Lord Scarman OBE

Frederick Muller
London Sydney Auckland Johannesburg

© Rod Hackney

The right of Rod Hackney to be identified as Author of this
work has been asserted by Rod Hackney in accordance with the
Copyright, Designs and Patent Act, 1988.

First published in 1990 by Frederick Muller
an imprint of Century Hutchinson Ltd,
20 Vauxhall Bridge Road, London

Century Hutchinson Australia Ptd Ltd
20 Alfred Street, Milsons Point, Sydney, NSW 2016

Century Hutchinson New Zealand Ltd
PO Box 40–086, Glenfield, Auckland 10, New Zealand

Century Hutchinson South Africa (Pty) Ltd
PO Box 337, Bergvlei 2012, South Africa

British Library Cataloguing in Publication Data
Hackney, Rod
  The good, the bad and the ugly.
  1. Great Britain. Architecture
  I. Title
  720,.941

  ISBN 0 09 173939 X

Photoset by Speedset Ltd, Ellesmere Port
Printed and bound in Great Britain by
Butler & Tanner, Frome, Somerset

To Tina and Roan
for their patience and understanding

Contents

Acknowledgements

This is my first book. Many friends and colleagues have helped. Special thanks to Lord Scarman, Bob Young, Nick Wates, Peter Womby, Charmaine Eatwell, Chris Hogben, Sam Webb, Ian Finlay, Charles Knevitt, Peter and Pat Elderfield, the Residents of my community architecture schemes in Macclesfield, Burnley, Stirling, Leicester, Birmingham, Millom, Belfast, Chesterfield, Carlisle, Cleator Moor, Manchester, Workington, Clitheroe, Longridge; to all those who live and lived in the Black Road Self Help General Improvement Schemes, past and present, especially June Daniels, Maureen and Hubert Higginbotham, Betty and Eric Hargreaves, Miss Madden, the Broadbent family, my immediate neighbours on Black Road, especially Mrs Heapy; all those in the Hawes Steet Residents' Association in Tunstall, Stoke-on-Trent, especially David Watkin and Carl Dawkins; to all those who work or worked in my various offices, especially to Moira Barron, Gennie Jones, Julie McAllister, Richard Gibson, David Quarterman, Chris Hesketh, Bernard Rushton, Michael Halsall, Jeremy and Honor Bell, David Gregory, David Andrew, John Kelsall, Teresa Borsuk, David Evans, Peter Kirkham, Paul Jozsa; to those helpers at the Royal Institute of British Architects, past and present, especially Pat Holmear, Bill Rodgers, Debbie Garrity, Chris Palmer, Alan Thompson, David Rock; to those who share in the concern for the inner city, HRH The Prince of Wales, Sam Springer, Bob Geldof, Canon Sebastian Charles; to those who helped with the preparation, especially Fay Sweet, Rowena Webb, Frank Delaney, and all those at Muller.

List of Illustrations

Foreword

In a very real sense this book is Rod Hackney's personal testament. His faith is in community architecture: his witness is set down succinctly and controversially. The careful reader will, however, note that, though he does not like some of the works of the 'Modernist' school of architecture, he does not deny the Modernists' achievements. Although Hackney challenges, even excoriates, some of the thinking and decisions of town and country planners since 1947, he believes in proper planning. And while he laments our cruel failure to lift the quality of life in the inner cities, he believes in an urban renewal that builds on what already exists and rejects demoliton to make way for some new architectural dream structure.

There is a melancholy note which constantly recurs in the development of his theme. It is that his own beloved profession has failed to bring the people for whom it has designed and built homes into partnership in the designing and building process. The concept of community architecture includes a design process during which architect, builder, engineer, and other craftsmen consult with their true clients, the people for whom they are building, and envisages preserving where possible the physical environment (e.g. streets, terraced houses, gardens, shops and pubs) by renewing, adapting, and improving existing structures. It is a concept of partnership between those who have the skills and those who need the homes. A substantial and fascinating feature of the book is its account of several community architecture enterprises in which our author used this idea of partnership to achieve genuine success.

Equally fascinating is the history of his own career as a student and architect. His professional education was dominated by the looming figures of the Modernist school (Corbusier and many others). His was a struggle to wrest himself free of their influence and power. But emerge he did as a practitioner of community architecture and as its very persuasive champion. He challenged the Modernists by standing for election as president of the RIBA and won. The citadel was stormed. In 1987 he found himself president and in a position to offer a very original leadership to his profession. It is a heartening story of enthusiasm and enterprise crowned by success.

You may well ask: is the Modernist to have no place in architecture? Is community architecture a panacea for all ills? My answer is that the Modernist has a genuine role: there are situations in which the function of a building calls for an original design or requires a dramatic or very grand statement of purpose. But it is another story when one is designing homes for people, ordinary men and women and their families. Rod Hackney has demonstrated that there is a crying need for community architecture in designing the living and working space of our people. If architectural design is, as I believe it is, a statement of function as well as the blueprint of a building, community architecture offers people the opportunity of having their say in the design which they want for living. I commend this book, and its author, to your attention.

Scarman
6 October 1989

1 The Making of a Modernist

I was born in Liverpool, shortly after the height of the Blitz, in 1942. Like all major British towns and cities, Liverpool suffered terribly from the combination of German bombs and wartime neglect. The resulting havoc and decay were to prompt some of the most significant changes ever to appear on the face of Britain. But as a small boy in the mid-forties I remained blissfully unaware of the way these changes would affect my later life.

My mother, Rose, was a dancer, and my father, Bill, was an hotel chef. As a family we soon left Liverpool, for my father's work took us all round the country. But when I was five he found a job in North Wales and bought a house in Bethesda, where we eventually settled. At school the lessons were given in Welsh, clearly a disadvantage for an English-speaking child, but the language barrier was eventually what led to my becoming an architect. I had to learn a whole new language, and not surprisingly, my written work suffered. But I always looked forward to art lessons, where there were no such problems; there, at last, I found a subject in which I could shine.

Before studying for my A levels there were the usual discussions about careers. I wasn't sure what I wanted to do, but my art teacher suggested that, because I was good at drawing and had an instinctive feel for perspectives and colours, perhaps I should become an architect. In the 1950s and early 1960s architecture was still considered an art, and skill at drawing was seen as a good enough reason to enter a course. Nowadays this has all changed. For example, maths is a requirement at A level; it wasn't for me. Indeed, I didn't even have maths at O level. My A level subjects were history, geography and art, and it was while studying for A levels that I decided to try my hand at an architectural career. I saw architecture possibly as an extension of the enjoyable and pleasurable art lessons at school.

When the time came I applied to Manchester University. At that time, the start of the sixties, Manchester and Liverpool were considered to be the top two schools of architecture in Britain, and so I knew competition would be tough. But I got a place, and in 1961 started my seven-year course. I was among the first students to receive a training devoted entirely to Modernism, which, with its revolutionary designs and use of new materials, seemed to provide the answers to so many current building problems.

Selling the dream

Britain was still in the grip of the post-war housing programme, and building was booming. Vast areas in the suburbs and city centres were being razed to the ground in a bid to conquer the squalor of the slums. Massive blocks were altering the skylines of almost every town and city.

The rush to build a new Britain for the twentieth century had begun immediately after World War I, when Lloyd George launched his massive 'Homes Fit for Heroes' project, which aimed to build 300,000 new houses. Each successive government had recognized that a large part of its sustained success and survival lay in building as many houses as possible as quickly as possible. In exchange for its votes, the population was offered the quantative solution for better living conditions.

After the urban destruction of World War II Churchill had tried to meet the desperate need for new homes. However, his attempts to drag a better Britain out of the rubble had failed, due to a shortage of supplies and a programme which was never fully developed. His plans were halted late in 1945 when the Labour Party came to power and announced its 'Operation Housing', under the charge of Aneurin Bevan. This was an early endorsement of standardized house building and the mass production ideas that we were to inherit – Churchill's plans had been simply an acceleration of the traditional house-building programmes carried out between the wars, relying on labour-intensive methods, accepting a rather slow production rate, and using the huge reservoir of manpower returning from the war to reconstruct Britain.

In contrast, the Labour government's programme was tackled like a military operation, even using wartime machinery – the Ministry of Supply, for example, converted its output from munitions to housing materials. The new styles, materials and town planning were seen as the only way forward in a country which, having prevailed against the wartime enemy, now had to take on the peacetime enemies at home – poverty and poor housing.

Amongst the new styles was that of the Modern Movement, which had begun with the German Bauhaus architects in the twenties and blossomed in Europe before the war. This particular method, which used the minimum of decoration, was seen by its protagonists as fundamental. To many of the new-thinking architects buildings such as Aarhus Town Hall in Denmark, built in 1939 by Arne Jacobsen and Eric Møller, made a refreshing change from the ubiquitous Gothic and Classical styles.

The new architecture appeared at first sight to be speedy and quick in production as well as flexible and adaptable in layout – hence its eager espousal by those who would rebuild the shattered Britain. But its use was limited immediately after the war because of its reliance on high technology and materials, like steel, that had become in short supply for anything other than the war effort. The period between 1945 and 1950 was therefore very much one of transition; for practical reasons building reverted to traditional form. All the while, however, the profession of architecture was gearing itself to mechanization, which would soon allow technology to flourish and make full use of the new styles and new materials.

Le Corbusier's vision

The war had been over for more than fifteen years when I went to university, but almost all building was still Modernist. It was a style and a philosophy admired by state and architects alike for its utopian vision. The designs and new materials also had the advantage of being quick and cheap. The architects associated with the Bauhaus, and Le Corbusier in particular, were the heroes whom our tutors encouraged us to emulate.

Le Corbusier's vision was beginning to be realized in Britain: 'Dwellings, urban and suburban, will be enormous and square-built; they will incorporate the principle of mass production and of large-scale industrialization. Our towns will be ordered instead of being chaotic.' Just as he predicted, small-scale, traditional methods of designing and building had been abandoned.

Local authorities throughout the land had admired and adopted Le Corbusier's neat plans and clear-cut solutions. La Ville Radieuse – a collection of drawings from 1935 demonstrating his ideas of zoning – provided a model which had been imitated all around the world. It showed towns built on a grid system and divided into zones for work, education, commerce, heavy industry and living. As students we knew that work lay with the local authorities after we qualified, and so we followed the Corbusian doctrine. If he and the councils wanted order, precision, standardization and industrialization, then so did we.

Towards a new architect

The role of the architect had also changed during the twentieth century. Before Modernism became fashionable the architect had been a universal man – a problem solver and a visionary equipped with a broad technical knowledge of how things worked, from an engine to an electrical system. He was a practical person who was not afraid to get his hands dirty. Joseph Paxton, nineteenth-century gardener to the Duke of Devonshire, railway promoter, developer, contractor, town planner and Member of Parliament, was just such a man. Born a farmer's son, he had no formal training as an architect, yet posterity remembers him for his brilliantly innovatory Crystal Palace, designed to house the Great Exhibition of 1851. Another of his schemes was for the Great Victorian Way, an 11-mile-long 'M25' around central London. The road was to be covered with a glass roof to reduce noise, and lined with houses, shopping arcades and public buildings; above everything would run a railway line.

The new-style designer, however, exemplified by Le Corbusier, was smart and chic with his sharp suits and round glasses. He could produce fine drawings and persuasive arguments for replacing anything old. Architecture had become a narrow discipline. Where once an architect would have had a thorough knowledge of design, engineering, planning and building, the job had shrunk to such a degree that he (a woman architect was rare) was seen as almost purely a designer – a cool, Corbusian character poised over a drawing desk creating tall, elegant structures. He would be heading a team supported by specialist engineers, planners and builders.

We young students were imbued with a great sense of our professional importance. Equipped with the new knowledge and ideals, we were being schooled to produce the new world. We were above criticism. This egotistical outlook was another Corbusian inheritance. His unflinching belief was that architects should be allowed to work without the hindrance of the public. Ordinary mortals, particularly clients, were in his opinion ignorant. 'A great part of the present evil state of architecture is due to the client,' he wrote, 'to the man who gives the order, the man who pays. We are all acquainted with too many big businessmen, bankers and merchants, who tell us: "Ah, but I am merely a man of affairs, I live entirely outside the art world, I am a Philistine." '

Le Corbusier's influence on students was powerful, not least because his copious advice, recorded in a series of books, was presented in stirring, revolutionary language. It was his unswerving conviction that exerted such a seductive appeal. His *Towards a New Architecture* was our Bible, and all students carried a copy metaphorically tucked under their arm:

A great epoch has begun.
There exists a new spirit.
Industry, overwhelming us like a flood which rolls on towards its destined end, has furnished us with new tools adapted to this new epoch, animated by the new spirit.
We must create the mass-production spirit.
The spirit of constructing mass-production houses.
The spirit of living in mass-production houses.
The spirit of conceiving mass-production houses.

That may all sound like empty rhetoric now that we have seen some of the results of the Modern Movement, but there can be no doubt of its good intention.

The Bauhaus School that was started by the architect Walter Gropius in Weimar, and later moved to Dessau, had strong socialist aims and attracted some of the greatest teachers of the time from a variety of inter-related disciplines. Their purpose was to spread their message throughout the world.

Lyonel Feininger, printer, graphic artist and writer, produced the Bauhaus manifesto's frontispiece, entitled *The Cathedral of Socialism*. Paul Klee, painter, graphic artist and writer, joined in 1921, followed a year later by Wassily Kandinsky, painter and graphic artist. The painter, theatrical designer, photographer, lithographer and typographer Laszlo Moholy-Nagy became a member of the Bauhaus in 1923.

In many ways the Bauhaus school's global thinking and belief in the marriage of the arts, both applied and fine, mirrored the thinking of William Morris and his friends. The important difference was that, unlike Morris, Gropius was not opposed to the use of machinery for the production of goods. Gropius believed, wrongly, that the machine would always be subservient to the will of the creator/designer – in the 1920s the world had not yet seen the damage that mass production could impose on individual design. The teaching of the Bauhaus was directed towards the mass production of objects such as teasets, which up until then had been mainly hand-crafted. Now only the prototype would be hand-crafted, and after that machines would mass-produce endless copies. The same would apply to buildings.

So the Bauhaus sprang from a sound philosophy. It was a reaction against Victorian and much turn-of-the-century design and architecture, seen by many an artist and architect as a hotch-potch of unblendable influences, lacking creativity or innovation. The Bauhaus members aimed to explore new materials and new techniques, and thereby offer more choice to society and free the expensive talents of the artist, craftsman and architect so that his skills could be concentrated on innovation and design, leaving the more laborious parts of his task to the machine. Little were they to know that the machine production process was to take on the fervour of a religious movement, being seen by politicians in particular as a godsend in producing cheap, mass-produced goods for ordinary people. Rather than the artist being in control of the machine, the machine was soon to dwarf the artist.

Building blocks

In the decade after World War II building stocks had been in short supply as investment in the home market had failed to keep up with demand. Britain's entire construction machine had been pushed to the limits and was struggling woefully to fulfil government promises to provide half a million homes a year. By the mid-fifties traditional building methods were considered slow, cumbersome and a hindrance. The only way to build new homes on a massive scale was by unrestrained use of the standardized, mass-produced materials advocated by the Modernists. A vast proportion of these systems had to be imported from France, Denmark and – ironically – West Germany. Entire rooms were shipped over and were then slotted together like Lego on site.

At university in the sixties we were instructed that time was of the essence. The world was moving fast and architecture had to keep pace. There was no time for reflection. Traditional construction methods using brick, stone, wood and slate were considered outmoded and were simply not taught. Belief in modern technology was very fashionable; disciples of the old school were considered fuddy-duddy. The radical rejection of the past was complemented by a blind faith in 'hip' modern building materials – off-the-peg panels, concrete, glass, metal, plastics and aluminium were our stock in trade.

It wasn't considered important to understand how the materials performed – that was the engineer's responsibility. If one dared question the long-term performance of the new, the reply was swift: in the same way that technology had developed the materials, it would also develop solutions to problems as and when they were required. It seems shocking now to consider that my only experience of handling materials was in the very first year of training, when balsa wood and clay were used in modelling exercises. Hardly materials which had widespread application in the outside world.

From the 1920s onwards, in his many publications Le Corbusier had predicted these changes and the rise of industrialized materials:

In the next twenty years, big industry will have co-ordinated its standardized materials, comparable with those of metallurgy; technical achievement will have carried heating and lighting and methods of rational construction far beyond anything we are acquainted with.

Contractors' yards will no longer be sporadic dumps in which everything breathes confusion; financial and social organization, using concerted and forceful methods, will be able to solve the housing question, and the yards will be on a huge scale, run and exploited like government offices. . . .

As the price of building has quadrupled itself, we must reduce
the old architectural pretensions and the cubage of houses by at least one-half; henceforth the problem is in the hands of the technical expert; we must enlist the discoveries made in industry and change our attitude altogether.

Construction has discovered its methods, methods which in themselves mean a liberation that earlier ages sought in vain. Everything is possible by calculation and invention, provided that there is at our disposal a sufficiently perfected body of tools, and this does exist.

Concrete and steel have entirely transformed the constructional organization hitherto known, and the exactitude with which these materials can be adapted to calculation and theory every day provides encouraging results, both in the success achieved in their appearance, which recalls natural phenomena, and constantly reproduces experiences realized in nature. If we set ourselves against the past, we can appreciate the fact that new formulas have been found which only need exploitation to bring about (if we are wise enough to break with routine) a genuine liberation from the constraints we have till now been subjected to. There has been a Revolution in methods of construction.

Less is a bore

The revolution in materials joined forces with the revolution in design. For us architectural students, class time allotted to the study of Classical styles and traditional pitched-roof brick buildings was minimal and treated as a straightforward historical exercise. The past was dead, and the only way was Modernism – although I know I wasn't the only student who filled the back of notebooks with drawings of cosy, stone- and brick-built houses.

We were being programmed to be good Bauhaus clones, and so our entire architectural education was focused on the minimal. In Mies van der Rohe's well-used catchphrase, we set out to prove that 'less is more'. We were taught to streamline, to strip away all excess (a design philosophy to which the Post-Modernist American architect Robert Venturi made the perfect retort: 'Less is a bore'). To the disciples of Bauhaus Classicism, and therefore ornament, was seen as decadent and bourgeois. The style was felt to imprison people because it was heavy, dowdy and dark; it was too domineering a form, and a drain on time and money. The only way ahead, we were informed, was to take a fresh look, to free things, to simplify, and to design light, bright, airy, hygienic, economic buildings which suited the age.

The early products of this thinking had been mostly stark, individual houses of a basic cube shape, constructed almost entirely of concrete and glass. The Bauhaus architects had experimented with brick and timber building, but later eschewed these old-fashioned methods after discovering the use of concrete as a structural material. It had been used only in the foundations of traditional buildings, but the Bauhaus builders seized upon its capacity to be poured and cast for walls, floors and flat roofs.

The wonders of Modernism were revealed to us through illustrations of particular projects, such as the early steel-framed and concrete houses designed by Muche and Gropius. There were also the Fagus factory, constructed of brick, metal and glass, and the Bauhaus's Dessau headquarters – a massive building, completed in just over a year, which testified confidently to the success of new materials and methods.

The link was made between modern needs and the answers

provided by modern design and technology. Everyone has heard Le Corbusier's adage that 'A house is a machine for living in.' Expanding his philosophy, he went on:

> An armchair is a machine for sitting in and so on. Our modern life has created its own objects: its costume, its fountain pen and its plate glass, the safety razor and the briar pipe, the bowler hat and the limousine, the steamship and the airplane.
>
> Our epoch is fixing its own style day by day. It is there under our eyes. Eyes which do not see.
>
> As to beauty, this is always present when you have proportion; and proportion costs nothing; it is at the charge of the architect. There is no shame in living in a house without a pointed roof, with walls as smooth as sheet iron, with windows like those of factories. And one can be proud of having a house as serviceable as a typewriter.

I must say that as a student of architecture I had great difficulty understanding the furore created by Le Corbusier's thinking. I simply couldn't see the point of publishing such complicated and untried methodologies for what should have been the simple task of erecting a shelter to keep the weather out.

I could see how impressive he was as a draughtsman but I felt that a lot of people at Manchester School of Architecture simply admired it as drawing for drawing's sake. To me, Le Corbusier seemed to be far better at idiosyncratic one-off buildings, such as the chapel at Ronchamp in eastern France. Here the use of sculptural form produced what I see as a Classical building of genius with a tremendous sense of place – a truly religious structure. This was where his genius was best employed, in buildings that lent themselves to individual expression, and not in the dangerous area of trying to produce mass housing for ordinary people.

Streets in the sky

As early as the twenties Le Corbusier was extolling the virtues of towers. His clinical vision was precisely what local authorities of the sixties and seventies dreamed of achieving with their tower block schemes:

> Dust, smells and noise stifle our towns of today. The towers, on the other hand, are far removed from all this and set in clean air amidst trees and grass. These towers, rising up at great distances from one another, will give by reason of their height the same accommodation that has up till now been spread out over the superficial area; they will leave open enormous spaces in which would run, well away from them, the noisy arterial roads, full of traffic which becomes increasingly rapid. At the foot of the towers would stretch parks: trees covering the whole town.

The mess of human activity irritated him. It didn't fit into the grand plan – he even described cafés as 'that fungus which eats up the pavements of Paris'. And in his *Manual of the Dwelling* he went so far in his fastidiousness as to prescribe how occupants should organize their interiors: 'Keep your odds and ends in drawers or cabinets. To keep your floors in order eliminate heavy furniture and thick carpets. Never undress in your bedroom. It is not a clean thing to do and makes the room horribly untidy.' This statement proves beyond doubt that Le Corbusier had no real understanding of human beings and therefore, by implication, was a totally inappropriate person to design homes. It is a trait he shares in common with a number of famous names in the architectural profession, especially those who see buildings as sculptures. Arne Jacobsen, for whom I was later to work, was sometimes moved to knock on the door of houses he had designed where he felt that the owners had ruined the façade with inappropriate soft furnishings. He would ask, for example, if they would mind terribly removing the net curtains. The reaction from the occupants can be imagined!

Le Corbusier's Unité d'Habitation in Marseilles, completed in 1952, was shown to us students as a model development. It was the first building designed in the deck-access style of streets in the sky – wide thoroughfares with apartments along one side. For many years Le Corbusier had been working on the idea of putting entire towns on stilts. At last he had achieved it in Marseilles by housing 1600 people in a unit which was virtually self-contained – there were also a shopping centre, children's nurseries, a gymnasium and artificial gardens.

The Unité was seen as the perfect answer, not just to housing vast numbers of people, but also to halting unruly urban development. Towers were believed to take up less space than streets (an idea that has since been proved wrong, since towers have to stand in large open areas in order to allow adequate natural light into flats).

The tempting prospect of saving space was welcomed with much enthusiasm in Britain, where land was at a premium. And the Marseilles block was soon duplicated on a smaller scale, just before I started studying architecture, with the prestigious Alton West estate in Roehampton, designed by London County Council architects, which was completed in 1958. Here Victorian town houses close to the edge of Richmond Park were demolished to make way for slab blocks in the Unité style, twelve-storey tower blocks and a cluster of low-rise houses. The demolitions had, however, left the landscape and trees intact, and so the new buildings were slotted in between the greenery.

Alton West was considered to be a huge success – the national newspapers and trade magazines ran stories proclaiming that the smart apartments offered everything required for modern lifestyles. They were light, hygienic, streamlined and set in the most beautiful surroundings. But Alton West was also the beginning of the blight. Architects and planners failed to recognize that good landscaping, meticulously maintained, is a necessary concomitant to tower block living. But if no landlord cares enough to keep the surroundings clean and tidy, even the most houseproud tenant gives up in disgust. Litter and vandalism breed more of the same.

My university lectures were geared to promoting all the new designs: deck-access blocks, tower blocks (also known as point blocks) and curious inventions such as the scissor block. This last design had a strange internal staircase system which meant that flats criss-crossed over each other: doors from each landing would lead downstairs to one set of flats and upstairs to another set. But no matter how the internal arrangement was designed, the exterior was uniform. Large, straight-sided buildings with flat roofs were the style, and all buildings – whether they were offices, airports, shopping centres, railway stations, cinemas or town halls – were treated in exactly the same way.

Brute force

A new generation of architects now began experimenting with the pioneer Modernists' tools. One of the most popular styles to emerge in the fifties was Brutalism; now we can see it as one of the most pernicious, because of its widespread adoption in British council housing. Brutalism found favour because it was so 'truthful' – concrete buildings could be built and left unclad, showing that the fascia was also the actual structural material. Different finishes were experimented with – the concrete was ribbed, beaten and even textured with a woodgrain effect.

In America, Paul Rudolph's 1963 Art and Architecture Building at New Haven was held up to us as a prime example of how powerful, exciting and violent raw concrete could be. Louis Kahn was probably the least compromising exponent of the school with his bleak block-style projects – a Unitarian church in New York, the Trenton Bath Houses in New Jersey, and the Salk Institute Laboratories in California. In sixties' Britain Brutalism bred contemporary heroes like Peter and Alison Smithson. The style took hold during my early student years when it was widely adopted by local councils for their tower blocks. State-funded Modernism was now introduced on a horrendous scale.

Throughout the fifties the Smithsons had taken Le Corbusier's ideas of streets in the sky and produced them in grey concrete. In turn their ideas sparked off projects like the massive Sheffield public housing complex of Park Hill by Lynn, Smith and Nicklin in 1961, which was hailed as brilliant. In the ensuing thirty years it has suffered some structural problems such as crumbling concrete, but has managed to achieve a measure of social success – possibly as a result of good relations forged between the city council and tenants.

In 1965, another ugly example of Brutalism was finished at Elephant and Castle – Ernö Goldfinger's Alexander Fleming House. Despite opposition from Modernists – its only admirers – plans are now afoot for it to be reclad.

One of the most famous, and one of the most heavily lambasted, examples of Brutalism came a decade or so later with Denys Lasdun's National Theatre on London's South Bank. Its vast concrete slab façades and walkways have since been a constant source of criticism, and it has frequently featured at the top of lists of most hated modern buildings. Plans were mooted by the Greater London Council to landscape all the bleak external areas of the South Bank, but these failed to reach fruition before the GLC's demise. Early in 1989, however, Terry Farrell proposed a scheme to breathe new life into the complex by encasing it in glass and introducing shops, a cinema, recording studios and cafés. This scheme will, I am sure, overcome some of the South Bank's ugliness. Some people think, cruelly, that the new plans are window dressing, but the South Bank certainly needs a little dressing up to overcome the bleakness and starkness of some of the individual buildings which occupy one of London's most visible and important sites.

Monuments to Modernism

Certain administrative changes also cleared a path for Modernism. There was a building boom, particularly in London, after the lifting of building licences in 1954. The wartime restrictions on commercial development were now swept away, and developers enjoyed a field day. So, not unexpectedly, did Modernism.

In 1962 the Shell Centre was constructed near Waterloo Station. It became London's tallest structure at 351 feet, but was quickly followed by the 287-foot Vickers Tower on the opposite side of the Thames at Millbank, and then the Hilton Hotel in Park Lane in central London at 328 feet. The capital's skyline was altered irrevocably.

The old City of London was subjected to a violent upheaval in 1964 when 13 acres of Georgian and Victorian terraces were cleared to make way for the Barbican development of high-density privately owned tower blocks along London Wall. The following year saw the building of Centre Point. The huge concrete tower in Oxford Street, erected by millionaire developer Harry Hyams, stood as the symbol of Britain's post-war property boom. Although it was to remain empty for fifteen years, it continued to increase in value because of rising land prices.

Outside London, Frederick Gibberd was busy throughout the sixties with work on Liverpool Cathedral. The design, which resembles a power station chimney (the building is known locally as 'Paddy's Wigwam' or 'The Mersey Funnel'), was constructed using sheet aluminium, concrete and stone. The large circular internal space is surrounded by columns and topped with a spiky metal crown. Basil Spence was working on another ecclesiastical building, the new Coventry Cathedral being built alongside the ruins of the old war-damaged one. This excited considerable interest because it involved the commissioning of various pieces of art – sculptures, stained glass, paintings and tapestries – and so was seen as a complete synthesis of Modernism.

James Stirling and James Gowan produced the Engineering Building at Leicester University, which was considered an unqualified success when it was built in 1964. It is an asymmetrical collection of shapes built of standard industrial parts – a tall brick and glass tower to one side adjoining a low-rise block, and an even lower glass 'shed' with odd projecting glass cubes on the roof.

Bad dreams

Despite the success of some of these buildings, the longed-for Utopia showed early signs of cracking up. Flat roofs often leaked and were inappropriate in Britain's wet climate. But the traditional pitched roof, designed to help rain run off, was rejected by our lecturers in favour of the flat simply because that was modern. We were even told that it was good for flat roofs to collect rain because the water would act as insulation!

Other structural problems soon came to light. During one student trip I visited the pre-war Quarry Hill flats in Leeds, designed by R. A. H. Livett, to learn about the ducted Garchy system, which allowed most kitchen waste to leave by the sink. Clever and innovative though their waste disposal methods may have been, the flats had started to fall to pieces. The seven-storey blocks had been built using the French MOPIN system – steel frames with reinforced concrete panels – but because of the poor-quality materials and lack of maintenance the steel was corroding, the foundations were becoming unsound, the concrete was crumbling and there was considerable damage through rot and damp caused by water penetration. Many tenants had asked to be rehoused. The block was later demolished, only forty years after it was built.

Early Le Corbusier schemes were also showing signs of decay, with crumbling concrete, staining and severe weather damage. One of his housing estates, at Chandigarh in India, was virtually

17

laid waste during the monsoon because neither the concrete nor the flat roofs could withstand the rain.

Modernist heroes

Such problems were, however, dismissed by our tutors as minor technical hiccoughs which could easily be remedied. Le Corbusier was still worshipped as a god, and the work of his disciples was treated with equal reverence.

Mies van der Rohe was one such mentor, and the influence of his work and style launched many of my fellow students in their careers. His fifty-eight-storey Seagram Building in New York, designed with Philip Johnson and completed in the late fifties, received universal praise from our lecturers. This great bronze-and-brown-tinted glass tower, nicknamed the 'Bronze Baby', was considered the ultimate in visual form and advanced engineering. Its aesthetic perfection meant that the blinds had to be automatically controlled – Mies was concerned that the beauty of the building would be spoiled if people in different rooms started pulling down blinds to different levels. The automatic controls failed to take into account that a person working inside could be dazzled by the sun and yet remain completely unable to draw down the blind. People in such a controlled environment tend to devise ingenious methods to overcome their problems: moving away from the window and providing home-made screens are just two approaches. A more extreme solution would have been quitting the job for a more congenial working climate.

Mies' Lafayette Towers in Detroit, completed in 1963, provided us students with an example of the most up-to-date use of curtain walling. And to show that he could handle smaller projects there was Farnsworth House in Illinois – a glass box sandwiched between two horizontal slabs of painted steel. The huge glass window expanses made it difficult to heat, but that wasn't considered a major drawback because fuel was cheap and it had, after all, been designed simply as a weekend retreat.

Frank Lloyd Wright was only admitted to the designers' pantheon by our tutors for his prestigious Guggenheim Museum in New York, the Price Tower in Oklahoma, and the Johnson's Wax Building at Racine, Wisconsin. His many designs for private houses, now considered among the most spectacular contributions to twentieth-century architecture, were only mentioned in passing. He was, however, treated with a degree of wariness because he had dared to criticize his fellow architects, and I could see that his type of Modernism didn't quite fit the norm. Now we know that most of his designs, although Modernist in inspiration, have stood the test of time. Frank Lloyd Wright's work has a genius which transcends the narrow Modernist idiom.

He was, in many senses, an individual. It may have been on his grandfather's farm in Wisconsin in the late nineteenth century that his special relationship with landscape and nature was forged: his designs for prairie houses were low and horizontal and kept themselves close to the earth. In the 1920s some critics thought his career had come to an end because he was being left behind by the new ideas of the Modern Movement; yet he then designed a number of superb modern buildings. He did not reject ornament, pattern and decoration, but even so some of his later work was deliberately uncompromising and designed to shock.

Unlike Le Corbusier, he had no inhibitions about the way people used his buildings and in the main he avoided falling into the trap of high-density, high-rise, heavy system building for working people, and it was this that was to save his reputation.

To me, it was his remarkably varied approach to architecture, never locked into one style, which put him on a pedestal above Mies van der Rohe, Le Corbusier, Gropius and, indeed, any other architect of this century. If he has to have a label attached to him, then perhaps Frank Lloyd Wright should be seen as an organic architect: all his designs were rooted in nature. He was a great draughtsman, a writer, a town planner, an engineer, an architect, a sculptor and a builder – another true universal man.

A voice in the wilderness

Apart from certain exceptions like Frank Lloyd Wright, I had started to have serious doubts about the architectural gods. I had seen that Modernist building was flimsy, badly built, and too often falling apart. The exclusive reliance on modern materials made no sense – it seemed inevitable that office blocks or schools made with walls of glass or plastic panels would be difficult to heat, that poorly sealed flat roofs would leak, and that concrete would soon become stained and ugly. Added to which so many of the designs seemed bland, soulless, often nonsensical and even occasionally threatening.

I had also begun to feel particularly uncomfortable about the destruction of neighbourhoods and town centres. But there was no forum for my criticism, and there seemed to be no time for questioning or doubting. Lecturers continued to deliver the dogma that Modernism would provide a better environment and insisted that the populace, once it had grown used to the styles, would appreciate the enormous contribution that architects were making.

My reservations remained, and while my fellow students were claiming the founder Modernists as role models I chose Thomas Telford. He was a great Victorian engineer and draughtsman who could turn his hand to building canals, roads and bridges, as well as housing. I wrote a thesis on the way Telford had worked, especially his management and political skills in getting schemes off the ground. His A5 London to Holyhead road not only required visual designs skills and much innovation on the design of the Menai Suspension Bridge between Anglesey and the mainland, but he also had to acquire land, train his workforce and draft parliamentary legislation to get the scheme underway. Having such a blatantly un-Modernist hero was just thought of as old-fashioned and eccentric.

Visiting the wastelands

My early doubts were reinforced with study trips. One of the first was to the vast concrete council housing complex at Hulme in Manchester, which, designed by Hugh Wilson and Lewis Wormersley with the City Architect's Department, was just being completed. I had known the area well as a child, and was shocked to see that 300 acres of old Victorian terraces had been flattened. The residents had been removed to Corbusier-style streets in the sky.

The Hulme estate was divided into six zones containing a mixture of houses and maisonettes, but mostly dominated by enormous deck-access blocks and towers. The *pièce de résistance* was considered to be Zone 5 – massive slabs of buildings arranged in semi-circles in an attempt to emulate the Georgian crescents of Bloomsbury and Bath. The crescents were named, ironically in view of their overwhelming ugliness, after great architects – Robert Adam, John Nash, Charles Barry and William Kent. At the time they were being built Lewis Wormersley had said:

We feel that the analogy we have made with Georgian London and Bath is entirely valid. By the use of similar shapes and proportions, large-scale building groups and open spaces, and, above all, by skilful landscaping and extensive tree planting, it is our endeavour to achieve at Hulme a solution to the problems of twentieth-century living which would be the equivalent in quality of that reached for the requirements of eighteenth-century Bloomsbury and Bath.

To me it looked nothing like Georgian Bath, and I am sure the names chosen by the City of Manchester for their crescents had the four architects turning in their graves.

In Zone 5, surrounded by thousands of tons of grey concrete, I was asked to keep faith with the Corbusian ideal. People were being rescued from the squalor of the past and given a new breath of life, order and light. Their 'improved' future lay in standardized flats with rooms of carefully calculated sizes, and they were granted the luxury of large public spaces for their recreation. The so-called landscaped areas seemed to be a desert. From almost the day they were built, the decline set in. Why, I asked myself, was most of the ground floor taken up with car parking on the outside of the curved blocks when hardly anybody seemed to have a car? Most of the garages on the ground floor were also unused, but blighted the whole level.

The Loughborough estate in south London was another enormous complex that we were taken to see. It had been laid out in a different style from Hulme: there were more blocks, smaller in scale than those I had seen in Manchester, and all set in less open space; but here again there was the deck-access idea of streets in the sky. Already signs of decay were evident – the Brutalist concrete was stained and unpleasant, several doors and windows were broken, rubbish bags lay uncollected, fences had been knocked down and the public areas were clogged with litter and fouled by dogs. The fortress design and concentration of huge numbers of people in such a small place gave the estate, even to a visitor, an intimidating feel. It had become a no-man's land in no time at all.

Visits to 'model' estates were followed by visits to so-called successful new towns – which had earned British architects highly respected reputations abroad. A new town was exactly that – built from nothing. Traditionally towns evolved – they grew in a rather haphazard way, mainly from the centre outwards. This presented no real problem until the industrial revolution; then in Britain between 1811 and 1851 there was a rapid rise in the numbers of people living in large cities.

Certain industrialists and philanthropists designed and built new towns and villages for their own workers. Robert Owen, founder of the Co-operative Movement, was responsible for what he called 'Villages of Co-operation', where a population of between three hundred and two thousand could be housed close to their work space. Industrialists such as Titus Salt with Saltaire in Bradford; the Cadbury family in Bournville, Birmingham; and Lord Lever with his Port Sunlight in Cheshire followed in this line of thinking. Raymond Unwin designed larger conurbations. Ebenezer Howard with Letchworth Garden City and Frank Lloyd Wright with his Broadacre Estate went a stage further. Both the latter two architects, however, unlike Le Corbusier, said that the design must be site-specific – in other words not drawn until the site is analysed, taking into account the individual topography.

Britain's post-war new towns – the ones people usually think of when they hear the expression 'new town' – included Welwyn Garden City, Harlow, Stevenage and Milton Keynes, and, in Scotland, Cumbernauld and New Irvine. The ideal new town when I was a student was considered to be Cumbernauld, designed by Geoffrey Copcutt, Hugh Wilson and D. R. Leaker between 1956 and 1961.

Cumbernauld, New Irvine and the burgh of Rutherglen were built as satellite towns to the city of Glasgow. New Irvine was also intended to exploit the largely unrealized potential of the coastline and thus create a new economy within this locality. Cumbernauld's New Town Development Corporation, on the other hand, aimed solely to serve the Glasgow metropolitan area, housing city workers who would have their own shops and leisure facilities and were expected to commute to work by rail, car or bus. (A new town development corporation is similar to a local council, the main difference being that the corporation is also meant to attract private finance, including shopping, for some of the commercial areas, and being a self-contained bureaucracy within otherwise rural surroundings it could single-mindedly concentrate on setting up a new town.)

Here at Cumbernauld we saw the practical application of Le Corbusier's Ville Radieuse – zoning, with residential blocks on the outskirts and a commercial centre perched on a hilltop. The whole place was bleak and windswept – a collection of square and rectangular concrete boxes alongside vast expanses of car parking spaces. The original idea of a single citadel-like structure stretching for half a mile, 200 yards wide and eight storeys high, had been curtailed to just a short stretch spanning the main central highway. Wilson and Copcutt's vision was to produce a town which was easy to add to or dismantle – flexible enough to cope with changing economic or social patterns. However, although that theory may have appealed as an abstract idea it would by today's standards be thought clearly lacking in any understanding of humanity.

The designs had been highly praised by architectural critics at the time. One, Robert Jeffrey, said the public had been given 'a new insight into the nature of urban architecture with layers meshed together by vertical shafts of circulation to give an experience of a city centre as an incredible interlocking of uses and values'. Maybe this is an experience that planners and architects think ordinary people would enjoy. In fact to an ordinary flat-dweller it simply sounds like gobbledy-gook, and what may appear very attractive on a planner's layout, on which designers can spend hours working out spatial relationships and interlocking communications routes, can be sheer hell for the people who have to use it. It doesn't matter how eloquent an architect's or planner's explanation in an architectural journal may be – he could well be describing an unworkable jungle which may cripple the lives of those who have to live and work in its hideous labyrinth.

I remember going into one of the penthouse flats above the shopping area in Cumbernauld to meet a resident. He had obviously been visited many times before by students and housing officials, and had all the right answers ready. He was a council tenant and would have liked the opportunity to buy his flat; however, he did concede it had faults. Living there was a lonely existence. He knew none of his neighbours and, once the shops closed, the place was deserted. The five exposed sides – three walls, roof and floor – also made it extremely cold in winter. The only thing this particular tenant seemed to look forward to were the frequent wide-eyed visitors to his flat. I wonder where he is now, after the propaganda has been replaced by the stark reality of a failed dream.

Each site, whether it was an estate or a new town, looked desolate. The smoggy atmosphere of the surrounding industrial cities had already stained the solid grey concrete façades, there was no sense of community, people spent as little time as possible in the streets or other public areas, the huge car parks lay almost empty apart from a scattering of old cars, and the shops were heavily fortified against vandals or burglars. But the accepted belief among my lecturers and the local authority officers to whom we spoke was that they were good places to live – they followed the ideals of Modernism and offered 'perfect solutions' to the housing problem. What ignorant assumptions, especially from people who left work at 5 o'clock to go home to a converted barn or modernised farmhouse. I wondered, though, why architects didn't live in their own mass-housing creations. Perhaps they simply didn't believe in them – the first sign of failure is when they lost faith in their own designs. Or was it more sinister – were these 'social' Modernist designers acknowledging that they were a class above those for whom they designed? So much then for all those Bauhaus beliefs in equality.

2 An Innocent Abroad

While still at university I had my first taste of working abroad, when I went to Canada in 1964. Cheap student flights were on offer in the summer holidays, and for £60 I set out for Ottawa. Before leaving Britain I had been promised a vacation job at an architectural practice called Murray and Murray. I was a fourth-year student at the time and, together with gaining some practical experience, I wanted to use my trip to complete a measured drawing exercise set by my tutors as holiday work. For this project I had chosen to visit Upper Canada Village – a timber-frame model village in Ontario which had been built to show visitors how the original pioneer buildings, such as houses and mills, had looked and were constructed.

However, when I turned up at the Murray and Murray offices they took one look at my long hair – which all British students had in those days – and told me there must have been some mistake. I didn't ever find out what they *were* expecting, but it clearly wasn't an English Beatle. I was given the sack before I had even started. Their reaction was a surprise and a blow – I was stranded in Ottawa with no money and had to find a job quickly.

After spending two weeks combing through the Yellow Pages I eventually found a job with a firm called Hart Massey. There I helped with several projects, including the building of a concrete-panelled university annexe. Massey and I got on well, and we worked together again when I returned to Canada at the end of my fifth year on the monorail station designs for the enormous Expo '67 exhibition project in Montreal.

Putting on a show

During the Expo, staged in Montreal, I was based in Ottawa and rented an apartment on the eleventh floor of a high-rise tower. It had the great advantage of excellent views – particularly of a drive-in cinema: I saw all the latest films, silent, but for free. Canadian efficiency was clearly demonstrated when, within four hours of moving into my tower, I was visited by the Bell Telephone Company asking me what colour telephone I wanted!

Living standards generally in Canada were higher than those I had left behind in Manchester. There was, of course, no war damage, and little sign of dereliction in the cities. Most buildings were well cared for, and the streets were clean. The availability of public housing was minimal. The pressure to provide huge numbers of local authority homes, as in Britain, simply did not exist in affluent Canada, which was in any case less densely populated. Most people lived either in city centres in the high-rise privately owned towers like mine, or in the timber-framed suburban houses.

British architects were well respected; the shared cultural similarities were clearly an advantage, and they had gained good reputations through the building of new towns – an idea eagerly copied in North America. The Festival of Britain exhibition in 1951 had also made a strong impression by alerting Canadians to European Modernist styles of building.

Montreal was wealthy and cosmopolitan and the site of some of Canada's most prestigious new buildings – all constructed in the international Modernist style. Mayor Drapeau had been intent on enhancing the city's worldwide reputation, and had encouraged architects from around the globe to design the major municipal and privately funded buildings. The one which struck me as by far the most outstanding was the Place Ville Marie, by the Chinese-American architect I. M. Pei. This towering, shimmering office block was built in a cruciform shape and clad in aluminium. It was unusual, impressive and, most importantly, well built.

The Expo '67 show was part of Mayor Drapeau's mission to transform Montreal into an international city. The exhibition was an ideal place for architects to show off; countries were invited to exhibit their latest designs and technology in national pavilions set in an enormous park on three islands in the St Lawrence Seaway. The Americans stole the show with their enormous metal and glass dome resembling a huge transparent golf ball, designed by Fuller and Sadao; Expo's high-level monorail ran right through the dome walls. The British missed their chance with an extremely dull pavilion design by Basil Spence, Bonnington and Collins. It was around 100 feet high, made of metal, and looking curiously like a ship's funnel pointing skywards.

My brief had been to design six monorail stations to last for the six-month duration of the exhibition – they are, in fact, still there more than twenty years later. The aim was to give the railway a feeling of lightness. The design was high-tech, and I used materials such as tubular metal for the columns, timber for platforms and canvas for the side panels.

It was a year during which I got to know a great deal about materials and styles: buildings in Canada had to withstand huge temperature changes, freak weather conditions and earthquakes. I also realized that the Canadians and Americans had a different approach from the British when it came to commissioning buildings. They displayed more concern about the final product, allowed generous budgets, and encouraged better design whether it was for housing or office blocks. The Canadians had the advantage of a buoyant economy and a smaller population than in the UK so there was less pressure to build quickly and cheaply, but I learned that Modernism could be successful when structures were soundly built with quality materials and well maintained.

All change

I returned to Manchester in September 1967 for my final academic year, in which our Modernist training was consolidated and we were encouraged to think bigger than ever. Each student was given a design project – most of these were vast schemes for hoverports, airports, large commercial centres and massive housing schemes. I chose to work on an idea that I had been thinking about for a long time – the possibility of converting Manchester Central Station into an exhibition hall. The idea was not greeted with much enthusiasm by the school. If I had been true to my teaching I should have been thinking about demolition and building something brand-new. What was the sense in spending just as much on a renovation scheme? However, I was allowed to go ahead and, indeed, my own tutor, Derek Dearden, was actively encouraging.

The beautiful Victorian building with its vast spans had been recently closed as a result of the recommendations of the Beeching Report on the state of Britain's railways. Beeching was responsible for the demise of so many lovely stations. It had soon become derelict, and now stood as an immense reminder of the recession in Britain's traditional industrial heartland. I had been inspired to take this project because of my work at the Expo – here was a chance to combine my newly acquired knowledge of designing exhibition spaces with the fascination for trains and railway buildings that I had had as a boy train-spotter at Bangor and Llandudno.

The station looked to me like an ideal exhibition space, and the battle that had just been fought over the planned demolition of the Euston Arch made it a topical subject. The famous Victorian arch, outside London's Euston Station, had been the focus of the first major conservation battle to be fought after World War II. Permission for its destruction was granted by Harold Macmillan's government in 1962; sadly the conservationists lost, and Philip Hardwick's elegant creation was destroyed. But the fight had at least drawn attention to our rapidly disappearing British heritage and the power of developers to get their own way.

In its hypothetical new role as an exhibition centre Manchester

Central had the tremendous advantage of being, as its name suggested, centrally located; and its situation next to the Midland Hotel meant that ample accommodation could be provided for visitors. The station also offered the chance for substantial underground parking in its two-storey maze of catacombs. And, despite the fact that it had been standing for over a century, the quality of the building was so high that it clearly had the potential to outlast all the surrounding Modernist structures. The Victorians didn't stint on materials or craftsmanship, and to have reproduced the technology used in creating the enormous spans would now have been prohibitively expensive. Manchester had a building of such superior craftsmanship that, if demolished, it would never again be replicated.

My plans involved a thorough overhaul of the structure, which would then be reclad in glass and metal panels. I also argued that simply turning the building into an exhibition hall would not, on its own, be sufficient to guarantee its success as a major attraction to exhibitors. The final brief for the building and its 26-acre site included restaurants, conference facilities, offices and a large grassed piazza. Around the outside I suggested there should be new offices and shops, with flats above. The idea was to create an area of mixed uses which could thereby attract considerable investment.

The suggestion of mixing housing with commerce and leisure jarred with the zoning principles of my tutors, but they were sufficiently open-minded to agree that the idea was basically sound. Ten years later I saw my plans come to fruition, when a similar scheme was completed and the station became the G-MEX exhibition centre and concert hall. It was officially opened by the Queen, who said in her speech: 'One of the problems facing the great cities of our country is what to do with the many vast monuments to our industrial past. There can be no better example of this problem, nor of how to solve it, than this fine old Central Station building.'

Unlike the Euston Arch, which was destroyed by greedy

commercial developers, Manchester Central was lucky enough to survive because the city did not have enough money to redevelop the site when conservation had still to become a powerful force in Britain.

Third world modernism

My second and final year abroad was in Libya between 1967 and 1968; here I was employed on a large, government-sponsored squatter resettlement programme. At that time the country was still ruled by King Idris, who was deposed by Colonel Gadaffi in a military coup shortly after I left.

Thousands of people from desert towns had made their way to the outskirts of the oil-rich cities of Tripoli and Benghazi, and the government had been unable to cope with such a massive influx. When I arrived in Tripoli the squatters had housed themselves in filthy conditions in an array of makeshift buildings – some lived in large drainage pipes, some in tin sheds and others simply under pieces of corrugated iron. Architects and planners were needed to bring a semblance of order and provide permanent homes.

The resettlement programme was divided into two parts – one provided industrialized buildings imported mainly from the Eastern Bloc countries, and the other, which I chose to work for, put up traditionally built homes. The job provided me with the best sort of training in the employment of building styles and materials but, most importantly, in understanding communities and people's needs. Faced with such a massive problem I had to forget large chunks of my training and adopt a completely different, pragmatic approach.

My work involved drawing up large proposals based on the usual Arab arrangement of placing homes around a central courtyard. They were single-storey, built with concrete blocks and then rendered; some were terraced and some were detached. The homes had to be designed to take account of other local customs, too. For example, the interior plan had to work in such a way that the women didn't have to mix with the men, and the courtyard had to act as an area for entertaining friends. Curiously, the only room customarily designed with an outward-facing window was the one reserved for guests. My traditionally oriented housing designs contrasted strongly with the imported prefabricated buildings being erected elsewhere in the area, which paid no heed to local customs.

Modern architecture in Tripoli was a great disappointment. The once-poor country had received a huge boost to its economy through the oil business. Much of this injection of new money was squandered on Modernist buildings. The city had seen its ancient quarters laid waste to make way for high-rise blocks; western styles were very fashionable and were imitated wherever possible. However, the industrialized systems based on units prefabricated in factories and delivered – often damaged – to the site were completely inappropriate for the country's climate. The air conditioning frequently broke down, making the buildings impossibly hot, and many had been badly damaged by the vicious desert sandstorms, known as ghiblies. These, at their most ferocious, could dump millions of tons of sand on the city in a matter of minutes. Traditional buildings were protected by wooden shutters and could withstand the storms, but the modern buildings emerged battered and sand-filled.

Some of the country's most beautiful examples of architecture were to be found in the desert and along the coastline. Leptis Magna and Sabratha were two almost perfectly preserved Roman towns. When the sea level rose in this area of the Mediterranean many towns were submerged and covered with silt and sediment; those that remained on land were covered with sand dunes. This, coupled with the fact that there had been no building here since Roman times, meant that, when excavated, the towns were seen to be superb examples of the Roman North African civilization. After World War II, when Libya received independence, the

ONE MAN'S VISION . . .

L'Unité d'Habitation, Marseilles. Le Corbusier

IS ANOTHER MAN'S POISON

Hulme Estate, Manchester

Libyans seemed to have no interest in Roman antiquity and, apart from a few tourists, the towns were hardly visited. When I went to see them the only signs of life were provided by a handful of stonemasons attempting restoration on a shoestring.

Danish lessons

After my year's work in Libya it was time to come back to England and find a job. On my return I spotted an advertisement for an English-speaking architect with Arab experience to work in Copenhagen with Arne Jacobsen, designing the Kuwait Central Bank. It sounded ideal. I was given a bizarre interview on the platform at King's Cross Station – the terminus where my busy interviewer arrived in London – and offered the job.

Denmark is a country with a solid design tradition, and it was plain to see that by educating people from early childhood an appreciation for good design stayed with them and paid off when they became consumers. Even in the most ordinary houses people had beautiful and carefully chosen rugs, furniture and lamps. Their colour co-ordination was immaculate, and there was a tremendous inbred sense of style and sophistication. From the first day at school children were taught how to appreciate good design – they were encouraged to experiment with colours and really look at buildings and objects around them. By the time they reached secondary school, therefore, they had developed a strong design sense.

People in Britain undoubtedly have the same instinct but, because design doesn't feature much in primary or secondary education, rarely have the means to articulate it: they will say something is 'nice', but won't be able to explain why. People like Terence Conran have to a certain extent opened the public's eyes a little over the last twenty-five years; but there is a long way to go before reaching the European and, particularly, the Scandinavian level of design appreciation amongst ordinary people.

As a result of the Danish system their children grow up to be visually literate adults and aesthetically educated clients who want the best architects. Modernism has not been allowed to ravage the country, and the majority of homes are built in good-quality materials and with traditional methods. The Danes haven't lost touch with their past and have the ability to recognize that when something is good it should be left alone. But to be fair, Denmark is, like Canada, a prosperous country with a small population, and therefore suffers fewer housing problems than the UK.

However, Denmark does have its drawbacks. The high living standards make it an expensive place. As an apprentice I was on a very low salary – about half that of a fully qualified architect – and so I was advised to live away from the city. I took a summer house in North Zeeland, near Helsingør.

A lot of people from the cities had second homes in the country because they loved the open air. These were often self-built, basic timber places ideal for weekends or summer visits. By contrast, homes in the cities were often dowdy-looking six-storey blocks of flats, but they were very well maintained and beautifully furnished. They were used from Monday to Thursday only, and then there would be a mass retreat to the country on Friday night to sail or walk and relax. The Danes had mastered the art of living in tower blocks because they knew they did not have to be in them seven days a week.

I was already familiar with the work of my new boss, Arne Jacobsen, since it had been shown to me at university as an example of what second-generation Modernists were producing. While he worked as a Modern Movement architect, he also had great respect for Classicism and tradition. Jacobsen was both talented and versatile: on one side of the street he could be designing a stucco and rendered flat-roofed house, while on the other side he could be working on a vernacular-inspired yellow brick equivalent.

The Søholm housing scheme, in which he himself lived, had

received massive publicity throughout Europe and North America during the late fifties and early sixties. The staggered form of the units, the sectional arrangements of the internal spaces and the style of the building were copied in many schemes by other architects.

His Munkegaard School also won great acclaim because it had been designed with children's needs specifically in mind – light switches at a low level, for instance, and easy-to-reach door handles. This also had its imitators. Munkegaard had been built at a time when the design of so many British schools used the industrialized CLASP system (a light steel and flat-roof frame with concrete panels clad in materials such as wood and hardboard), and so it provided a welcome departure from the received wisdom that mass school programmes could only be effected by the use of off-the-shelf building materials.

By the time I began working for Jacobsen he had established an international reputation – although some of his larger, more experimental projects had failed to reach the level of architectural quality he had attained in his smaller-scale schemes. His design for the Bellevue Theatre in Copenhagen, for example, had been heavily criticized by the client because, although it was intended to be functional, it spawned a whole range of technical problems. Jacobsen had designed a sliding roof to allow in light and air during the summer, but this frequently leaked when it rained. His designs for signs also came under attack – not unreasonably, because they were difficult to read. His forays into large sculptural structures also failed to work. The town centre scheme at Castrop Rauxel in West Germany was typical: the spread of buildings was far too extensive to be perceived as the sculptural entity he had intended. Like so many Modernists, Jacobsen was seduced into producing on a large scale when in fact his great strength lay in developing smaller projects.

The Kuwait Central Bank, on which I was to assist him, was at the time the world's most costly building, with its gold-leaf dome and vaults built to withstand nuclear attack. The structure was five storeys high, built in a combination of stone, granite, concrete, glass and aluminium. The interior was based around a central atrium running through four floors and sitting in a sea of light, above which was the top-floor conference room. The banking hall was placed inside the base of the atrium, and from there rooms led off for staff. The massively reinforced basement held the vaults, and here security was at its most sophisticated: strategically placed mirrors ensured that guards could watch the entire space at once, and every conceivable electronic security device was installed. The armoured doors were the most expensive ever made.

Jacobsen enjoyed the company of young people and liked to show off his design flair to them. He was not particularly interested in the Kuwait Bank building – an altercation on a previous commission from a Muslim country, the Pakistan parliament building, had led to his withdrawing from the project; apart from checking the designs produced by those of us who were now assisting him, he left us to get on with the task. On the whole he disliked the limelight, despite his huge international reputation.

Unlike most British architects, Jacobsen didn't restrict himself to working solely on buildings. He used his skills to design anything from tables and bathroom tiles to chairs, carpets, curtains, cutlery and even light fittings or landscapes. He believed in the architect as a universal man – a designer who could turn his or her hand to anything. This idea was one of the strongest influences on me and was one of the things I brought back to England with me in 1971, although it hardly earned me plaudits.

I wanted to write a PhD thesis on Jacobsen's work, and with £1000 in savings I headed once again for Manchester University.

3 The Dream Becomes A Nightmare

It was a changed Britain to which I returned: in just four years many towns and cities had been transformed. The guts had been torn out of them, and new building had been carried out at an alarming rate. The ugliness in contrast with the serenity of Denmark made my sense of shock all the greater. Whole areas were unrecognizable – acres of terraces had been razed and replaced by new tower block estates. In the city centres, where I remembered rows of individual, small old shops, there were now concrete slab precincts. All sense of scale and perspective had been lost.

It was not only the look of these places that had changed. People's attitudes had, too. They had begun to protest against their new homes and environments. In Denmark I had grown used to informed dialogue between the public, architects and the state. In Britain there were two simultaneous monologues – the public in opposition to official policy. Faith in the state machine and the better way offered by Modernist architecture had been badly shaken.

The beginning of the end

The turning point had come with the Ronan Point disaster in London. Just minutes before 6 a.m. on 16 May 1968 a gas explosion had ripped through the twenty-three-storey council tower in Newham, in the East End of London. One enormous panel of the concrete system-built block had been blown out, causing an entire corner of the tower to collapse. Five people were killed and eighty more injured.

The tower's builders, Taylor Woodrow-Anglian, had used the Larsen-Neilsen system of construction – a method which had no skeletal structure but was built by 'hinging' together huge concrete slabs for walls, floors and ceilings. The displacement of one slab had resulted in a complete loss of structural strength, and had caused the building to tumble like a house of cards. Taylor Woodrow-Anglian alone had built around forty similar towers in London and over six hundred in cities around the country. Thousands of people living in blocks felt vulnerable and helpless; they began to fear for their lives.

The disaster received widespread media coverage. For the first time, residents found an outlet for their complaints. They voiced their anxieties about the brutal, impersonal and often violent environment, and described the most dismal living conditions. Damp, condensation and vermin infestation were not isolated complaints.

Architects and engineers said the explosion was a fluke – Taylor Woodrow-Anglian even claimed that the construction method had prevented more damage than would have been caused in a traditional structure. But in addition to doubts over systems buildings, Ronan Point had also exposed the poor-quality workmanship, which was rife. Joints were badly made, newspapers and cement bags had been stuffed into crevices in place of bonding materials, and the concrete was cracking badly. On behalf of local residents, architect Sam Webb carried out a lengthy investigation. When he revealed the shoddy building practices the tower's caretaker said simply: 'That's piece work.' During the busiest building years construction workers had been given bonuses to complete jobs quickly, and so, as Ronan Point proved, instead of waiting for the delivery of parts they had improvised to earn more money.

The local council stood its ground. Breaking its ongoing

commitment with Taylor Woodrow-Anglian could have left them vulnerable to heavy penalties for breach of contract. So the council defiantly continued to pursue its construction programme throughout the year, until a Ministry of Housing report on the disaster was published in November.

This report revealed that, because of its weak joints, the Larsen-Neilsen system was susceptible to collapse as a result of wind, fire and any small explosions. It attacked the lack of research into modern materials and architects' inadequate safeguards as well as poor supervision of the builders. Soon afterwards a nationwide investigation was undertaken into all high-rise tower systems. The results showed up a wide range of structural faults, and many councils were forced to spend hundreds of thousands of pounds in strengthening their blocks. The massive council rebuilding programmes, particularly those comprising towers, gradually began to slow down, and during the early seventies almost all system-building firms closed.

In 1953 local councils in England and Wales had built around 7000 high-rise units. By 1968 that figure had changed dramatic-ally to 30,500. As a result of Ronan Point, by 1971 the picture had radically altered again with the construction of only 8000. But, despite the fact that fewer new towers were being built, there were many thousands still standing which were almost universally loathed by their occupants.

Towers of Babel

The early seventies witnessed a new mood of defiance. People already living in towers began to join forces to demand an option – they wanted to be rehoused. Others still living in their terrace homes tried to find ways of stopping the demolition programmes.

Local authorities were in a state of panic. Most were still repaying the heavy loans taken out to construct the towers. Their grants for new building were being cut; and as very little had been budgeted in the 1960s for repairs and maintenance, there wasn't enough around to look after and maintain the recently completed buildings. Local authorities receive Rate Support Grant and other allowances from the Exchequer which make up the difference between what they receive from local residents in rates and what they require to complete their housing and other programmes. When central government wanted to encourage local authorities to build, as it did in the 1960s, a lot of money was provided by it; when central government wanted to cut back, it simply reduced the amount of subsidy available. Most of the government money was given in the form of grants, which local government had to pay back over sixty years, with interest – very similar, in fact, to an ordinary mortgage taken out by an individual householder with a building society.

In Manchester at this time there was a substantial growth in activity by residents' groups, who were determined to keep their terrace homes and resist yet more slum clearance. They were in the prime target areas close to the city centre – Ladybarn, Fallowfield, Withington and Didsbury – adjacent to where the state bulldozers had already crushed almost ninety thousand homes.

Hitler hadn't caused a fraction of the destruction which followed in his wake under the guidance of Alf Young – Manchester City Council's energetic chief public health officer. Like most other city officials nationwide Young obeyed the letter of the law, which dictated that anything built before 1919 was by definition a slum and had to go. The buildings had reached the end of their useful life and had to be removed to make land available for the planners and their huge estates at Hulme, Moss Side, Ardwick and Beswick. This policy of mass demolition was meant to be halted with the 1969 Housing Act which, because of money shortages, was designed to encourage renovation of existing buildings. But its efficacy was not immediately felt.

The mood had changed at Manchester's School of Architecture. A group of students including Chris Taylor, who later became an architect in Leek, Staffordshire, Charles Knevitt, now architectural correspondent of the *Times*, and myself set ourselves up as advisers for residents' groups who wanted to save their homes. We made it publicly known that, if they were aggrieved about official policy and demolition, we would carry out informal surveys to be used at public inquiries, and help them in any possible resistance to the local authority.

We were also invited to visit some of the estates that had been built in the previous decade. I was horrified. The creation of a dependency culture, with more and more people relying on state subsidies and hand-outs, had left them powerless. The dream had turned into a nightmare.

Sinking fast

Hulme in Manchester was a typical example, and the early doubts I had experienced during my visit as a student seven years before were confirmed and amplified. Once the subject of praise as the largest urban renewal project in Europe, Hulme had disintegrated into squalor and decay – it had become a microcosm of all that was wrong with Modernism.

Before the bulldozers moved in, the 300-acre area had been crossed by a network of Victorian terrace streets. It had been full of charm; the homes were well built and attractive, despite being run down. Being old properties they lacked modern amenities and had suffered from wear and tear. Very few had proper kitchens – most had only a Belfast sink and a wooden draining board; some had no electricity supply, relying instead on gas lighting; very few had bathrooms. Most houses backed on to a cobbled rear yard with a shared clothesline, shared washhouse and shared toilets. There was a constant problem with damp coming down from the roof, in through the walls and up from the ground.

To the local authority public health inspector they were simply a blot on his portfolio of properties, and to him the best way of dealing with the situation was demolition. The city council pursued the Corbusian vision. It wanted to replace what it saw as the cramped mess of the terraces with vast, concrete, crescent-shaped blocks set in open, grassy areas where contented families could push their prams, walk dogs and take picnics.

The reality now was very different. As with the Loughborough estate in London which I had visited when a student, time had taken its toll at Hulme. The outside areas were unkempt, frightening, windswept places strewn with litter, glass and broken furniture, and fouled by the dogs that people kept in their flats to ward off intruders. Inside there was a prison atmosphere. The concrete had become stained and unsightly, some flats had been burned out as a protest against the council, and the lifts, stinking of urine, frequently didn't work. The long corridors and dark corners were terrifying at night. The only people giving awards and plaudits to architects now were the muggers and burglars. They appreciated how the Modernist designs afforded them ample hide-aways, alleys, and dingy hangouts. Just think how lucky architects have been never to have to account for themselves in court as accessories before the fact.

Notice to quit

The original residents of Hulme had been the usual mixture of working-class city dwellers. Previously the majority had lived as families in the old terraces – some were home owners, some were renting from private landlords, and some were local authority tenants. Their expectations of life had been at a low ebb in the post-war years when they were already suffering unemployment and hardship. But despite the problems there was always a strong sense of community. The first stage in the destruction of their lives came in the late fifties when notices were posted through letterboxes from the city's health department.

The story was the same all over the country – the city council announced its intention to 'improve' the area, which meant demolishing the old homes and replacing them with towers. There was no turning back. It was one of the biggest mistakes of the century – with the promise of better living conditions local authorities had ransacked whole neighbourhoods and taken control of housing out of the hands of residents. But the scale and cost of that responsibility was never anticipated. Wheeling and deali͏ ͏to bring plans to fruition was carefully calculated. Councils wer͏ ͏ ͏within closely controlled budgets. They needed to ac͏ ͏velopment at the lowest possible costs, a͏ ͏d houses had to go.

͏ ͏s deliberately to deflate prices. This was
͏ ͏blight on the area. Once 'improvement'
͏ ͏ulated, most homes were declared unfit for
͏ ͏cal authorities were obliged to pay market
͏ ͏w that as soon as their plans were announced
͏ ͏t property prices would plummet. Compulsory
͏ ͏s was then possible at a cut price. Both owner-
͏ ͏ndlords were powerless: they couldn't sell on the
͏ ͏d so the council's well-laid plans were assured of

͏ ͏erceptive and able residents knew how to spot the
͏ ͏s and prepared to take any action necessary to avoid
͏ ͏n a tower. Despite being unwilling to leave friends and neighbou͏ ͏s, the threat of the blocks was enough to persuade them to go. The luckier of the elderly residents left to live with relatives. This was the first exodus.

The downward spiral had really begun when around 20 per cent of those original inhabitants had fled and the important community balance was lost. Minority groups made up most of the rest, including the elderly, the unemployed, single parents, the mentally and physically ill, and ethnic families. Drug addicts and alcoholics would follow later. By the time of the move, the mix of residents

The picture caption which reads: 'The Arndale Centre, Manchester' should read: 'Hulme, Manchester'.

was way out of proportion to that in any normal community. Their demands on the council's services would be heavy.

The rot sets in

For the first few years on the new estates, life in the blocks remained more or less stable. This calm, in effect, lasted for just as long as the council managed to sustain adequate maintenance – ensuring that the lifts worked, the grass was cut and repairs were undertaken promptly.

The rot really set in when the place acquired a stigma. With spates of break-ins, muggings and the general physical decline of the building and its surroundings, the quality of life was threatened and residents began to feel intimidated by bullies. They were insecure in the lifts and corridors, and even inside their own homes.

Certain flats soon became vacant. Problems with lift mainten-ance meant that those flats at the top of the tower were least desirable – squatters or dossers moved in. The ground floor was also left empty because of its vulnerability to attack. Residents asked for transfers to the first, second and third floors because they were easy to reach by the stairs and allowed a quick escape in case of fire or violence.

Neighbourliness had disappeared. The old community had offered some support to those less well-off or ill. It was almost self-governing, because everyone knew their neighbour and some-body stepping out of line would be watched. The streets could also cope with small-scale change such as one or two people moving home a year, because it still left the majority knowing each other. But at Hulme, as at estates elsewhere, the community had been so badly disrupted that people were wary of others. The feeling of hostility was so great that residents preferred to remain anony-mous so as to avoid possible aggravation and confrontation.

When people got out of the lifts they made straight for their front doors and locked themselves away. It was not unusual to spend months in a block and never see your neighbour even on the same landing. Le Corbusier's notion that a street atmosphere could be nurtured in the sky proved a desperate and tragic mistake.

Order and maintenance crumbled. Policing on the estates was always notoriously difficult, time-consuming and costly. Many councils were forced to hire private security firms, but still vandalism and crime were rife. Councils took for ever to attend to repairs. The system had become ensnared in bureaucracy. First the local authority had to be called, then the message was passed to the maintenance department, and eventually the relevant engineers would be notified. Even replacing a window in a tower was a major task compared with replacing a window in a terrace house.

Refuse collection was frequently blighted. Chutes presented problems because they were often too small to take a full sack of household rubbish, and so alternative methods of disposal had to be found. Broken lifts left three choices – residents either wrestled with sacks down the stairs, left them on landings or, worst of all, threw them over the side to burst open and scatter on the ground. If the sacks did find their way to the collection points, there were still problems. Fires were common – often started by kids throwing lighted matches down chutes – and the collection points were so badly designed that it was difficult to drive refuse lorries up close. As a result, more spillage and mess were created.

The deterioration of the environment continued. Rain and wind battered the blocks and blew hard through the tunnels created by the long passageways. Graffiti, usually spelling out pure anger, frustration and aggression, covered the walls. Urine and excrement fouled the lifts and walkways. Teenagers often used those walkways as racetracks and screamed along them on motorbikes, daring each other to clock up record speeds. People coming out of their front doors have been knocked down and killed by motorbikes ten floors up.

Noise had always been a source of complaint. Some block designs actually amplify sound, particularly those where walkways are placed over bedrooms. The sound of footsteps echoed around flats; loud music also carried through the walls and floors. Local authorities' noise control units were ineffective. By the time they arrived the disturbance was over. Privacy was constantly invaded.

Lighting was inadequate and bulbs were not replaced. Heating systems failed with predictable regularity; they took ages to repair because of the long wait for ordered parts. Condensation and dampness were unavoidable because the solid concrete walls rarely dried out. Burst water pipes on high floors wreaked havoc and lifts, once broken, remained inoperable for weeks.

There was widespread rat, cockroach and flea infestation. Rats seemed to thrive by eating plastic pipe insulation and were abundant in Hulme. Cockroaches lived in the ventilation systems. Fleas spread behind wallpaper and timber skirtings. All were difficult to eradicate. Fumigation was easy in a Victorian house, but with large blocks all the flats linked together in one area had to be evacuated before any treatment could be administered.

Those residents who felt strongest set fire to their flats in a dramatic bid to be rehoused. Others refused to pay their rent. They knew that if they were taken to court they could explain their case and might stand a chance of being moved.

The bad name of Hulme was endorsed every time there was a crime in the centre of Manchester, because police immediately headed there as the most likely home of criminals. A ghetto atmosphere was generated, with police cars screeching round corners, lights flashing and sirens blaring.

Soon the estate became a no-go zone. Postmen refused to make deliveries, television engineers wouldn't call to make repairs, and residents became ostracized by shopkeepers and other local people. Once the place's reputation had reached rock bottom it was labelled a 'sink' estate – the end of the line. Councils usually offered people three choices of accommodation – the sink was the last. No self-respecting family would live there.

By 1971 many people had begun to vote with their feet: they had reached the end of their patience and moved out. It was preferable to stay with relatives in a cramped house elsewhere in the city than to have their own piece of modern architecture which conformed to the recommended Parker Morris standards on size. The local authority fought hard to keep up with repairs, but it was a losing battle.

The residents lost control over many areas of their lives. Old homes and neighbours were gone. They fell into debt when faced with higher rents and enormous bills for heating they didn't want but couldn't turn off because it was centrally controlled for the whole block. Many became ill with depression, or bronchial problems caused by the damp, and they lost sleep because of the noise.

They had become unwilling and unwitting guinea pigs in a state dependency support system; they felt looked down upon because they had to rely on the local authority for help. Eventually the tenants stopped complaining. Their silence was a frozen violence, which was eventually to erupt in the horrific riots of 1981 and 1985.

Shoddy practice

Commercial centres of cities were in as much of a mess as the housing estates. Money and power were the driving forces behind building projects. The more councils could build, the greater their reputations would be, was the firmly held belief. They enlisted the help of developers in order to speed up the process, and as early as the mid-sixties Britain boasted more than a hundred property millionaires.

The concept of the client as patron of the arts was seen as outmoded and therefore sacrificed. In Victorian times the best materials and craftsmen were used to create anything from factories to hotels as objects of beauty and permanence. Individual clients wanted splendid buildings, and while time has always been money, expediency and economy did not combine automatically to sacrifice quality. Architects were encouraged to produce major public and industrial buildings of distinctive personality to reflect the wealth and status of their clients.

But no council wanted to run a city still rooted in Victorian values. Each pursued a new image to demonstrate its prosperity. There were egos at stake, and the modern way flattered them. As in housing, industrialized systems were employed for shopping centres and offices. Many techniques were adopted. One involved the use of cladding materials which had no relationship to the structure; the walls, although appearing strong, had no load bearing. Tiles and even bricks were sometimes used simply as a visual expression rather than for their structural strength. Design input was minimal and almost exclusively Modernist. Quality was sacrificed for speed and, not surprisingly, the results were cheap and shoddy. Planners and highway engineers had a field day – wrecking old town centres and driving main roads through the intimate hearts of cities. Councils had tasted power. They liked it. Buildings sprang up as personalized memorials to individuals' conceit – but they were not structures of any design merit or lasting quality.

Power games were played to the limit – the most notorious being the Poulson affair. This received the most strident publicity because the dealings of architect John Poulson were exposed through a long-running bankruptcy hearing. He had used numerous contacts in local authorities, central government, clubs and public bodies to help clinch building deals. There were bribes and pay-offs, and his practice, based in Pontefract in Yorkshire, had become one of the largest in Europe.

Poulson was recognized as a designer of minimal talent, but he knew how to play the system. His unscrupulous dealings resulted in the rebuilding of massive areas of the North of England. He managed to secure multi-million-pound deals for everything from shopping and leisure centres to offices, hospitals and schools. The repercussions were wide-ranging, and brought about the fall of a cabinet minister, the collapse of the Labour Party in the North East and the imprisonment of T. Dan Smith, one-time Labour leader of Newcastle City Council. But when I returned to Britain in 1971 Poulson's work was still in progress and the full story had yet to be uncovered.

The politics of local authority architecture had become much more complicated than at any previous time. Building work was ruled by council committees, composed of elected members advised by planners and engineers, and architects had to spend more time and energy satisfying the bureaucrats than producing good designs.

Council planners wielded a strong influence. They were usually trained as geographers, and so had little design education or appreciation. Where was the sense in giving young planners the power to advise on the merits of an innovative multi-million-pound scheme when they were unable to make a qualitative judgement? Instead there was an obsession with minutiae like pavement widths, kerb heights and door sizes. And they saw it as their duty to keep a close check on building works to ensure that they complied strictly with the regulations. So, despite the 1947 Planning Act – which encouraged the emergence of the profession of planners as specialist geographers – there was no specific encouragement of original design. A safe and suffocating, boring universal style was adopted by architects as the key to obtaining planning permission. It appealed to the lowest common denominator.

Architects were also at the mercy of developers, who held the purse strings. Quality work cost money. Developers were well aware that maximum square footage could be achieved at a cut price using concrete and curtain walling. Any reference to the past which called for skills and craft was duly ignored. So much damage might have been prevented if only the more conscientious professionals had been brave enough to criticize the developers' working methods and materials.

Savaged cities

Birmingham had been an elegant if dirty Victorian city, but it had the misfortune to be wealthy during the sixties. Its industries were thriving. There was plenty of money in the corporate coffers to invest. The results were windswept plazas, desolate shopping streets and ghastly, faceless curtain wall office towers, the Holiday Inn, the Albany Hotel, the Post Office Tower, the new Bull Ring, countless roundabouts and intrusive road systems, including the most notorious with its derogatory nickname 'Spaghetti Junction'. The entrance to the rebuilt New Street Station should have been an impressive landmark as the major railway terminal of the Midlands. Instead it was given an insignificant entrance and built under-ground, denying the opportunity to give it a concourse. The new Birmingham sacrificed the pedestrian to the motorist, and made itself a concrete monument to Mammon and muddle.

Other cities, like Glasgow, were much more fortunate in being poor at the time. It couldn't afford a massive rebuilding pro-gramme, and as a result retains a wealth of old buildings. Twenty years later Birmingham is indulging in a second redevelopment exercise. Had the original buildings been saved they would be considered city treasures, and in the nineties would provide the focus for any urban redesign. Alas, few quality buildings apart from the Classical town hall were left standing.

Manchester had never been as wealthy as Birmingham, but none the less had failed to resist the lure of Modernism. It had been one of Britain's finest cities, with huge numbers of good-quality buildings erected in times when artistic patronage did not stint on expenditure. By 1971 a number of grand old buildings were decaying, and others, like the superb terracotta Refuge building in Oxford Street, and the town hall, one of the finest pieces of Gothic Victorian architecture, were being threatened in the name of progress. Fortunately both were eventually saved.

Meanwhile the Piccadilly Plaza, built in the sixties – again after the removal of solid Victorian masterpieces – was already showing signs of decay. Construction sites were in evidence throughout the city and considerable commercial building was in progress, concentrated on the central Market Street area which was dominated by the Arndale Centre shopping complex. This prestige project was one of the largest inner city shopping schemes in Britain – yet the design, consisting of a vast slab finished with tiling and bare concrete, resembled nothing so much as a huge public lavatory.

Looking at the new-style Britain, I felt a profound sense of loss. It wasn't simply nostalgic sentiment for familiar buildings. Old skills and intimate knowledge of materials had been abandoned, communities had been shattered, and so much money had been squandered in creating a wilderness. Britain, through its architecture had become cheap, shoddy and utilitarian. What a waste.

4 The Battle of Black Road

The refusal of a simple request for a £20 grant to fit a washbasin inside my house in 1972 sparked off a chain of events which were to change my thinking irrevocably. I owned and lived in a basic, perfectly sound, terrace house. But the local council decreed that it was in a slum area and was likely to be pulled down to make way for new development. At that time homes lacking basic amenities were seen by the council as unfit for human habitation. And because of that pronouncement, there was no chance of getting an improvement grant. But I had the benefit of professional expertise, and with that as our weapon my neighbours and I embarked on a two-year battle with officialdom and blinkered thinking.

The man who went to war over a washbasin

My first task on returning to Britain from Denmark had been to find somewhere to live. My search started in Manchester, where I would be preparing my PhD thesis. It didn't take long to realize that my savings, totalling £1000, would simply go towards paying two years' rent for typical student accommodation; that seemed like throwing hard-earned money down the drain. At that time housing in the area was cheap to buy, so I investigated the possibility of finding an old, run-down property. I had also returned from Denmark with a car, which meant I could easily live outside the city. After scouring the whole area to the east and south of Manchester, eventually I came across a reasonable property about seventeen miles south of the city, in Macclesfield. No. 222

Black Road was a simple two-up, two-down house built in 1815 as part of a terrace for local brick factory workers.

This particular house was in better condition than others in the road, and it was being sold furnished. I didn't own anything, so it was a great opportunity. The house itself cost just £300, plus a further £700 for furniture and fittings. Although that meant all my savings were used up I decided that after two years, when I was due to finish my thesis, the house could be either improved or resold.

There was one drawback. I had been warned by my solicitor that the property was subject to demolition plans. Macclesfield Council was busy with a project to knock down 800 houses as part of a slum clearance programme, and that included the Black Road area. I managed to get hold of a *Macclesfield Express* cutting dated 1968, which mentioned that the council's medical officer of health had submitted a report on 140 houses in Black Road, stating they were sub-standard. My house was among those surveyed, but at the time I was considering buying the council decision to demolish had yet to be declared.

The corporation was proud of its modern approach. In the previous five years it had completed a number of big block schemes, including two tower blocks at Hurdsfield and a deck-access scheme near the railway station at Victoria Park. The results had been hailed as a success by the local press, and the council was determined to repeat this great work. (Despite the accolades which greeted the Victoria Park scheme, it wasn't long before it went the way of most others around the country.)

I decided to buy the property in spite of the solicitor's warning. Even if the area was cleared, I reasoned, I could live there for two years while completing my PhD and then perhaps get some compensation.

All the Black Road houses were basic, to say the least. My immediate neighbours had one outside toilet shared among six homes, and one washhouse shared among ten. Water was laid on to those few houses that had a Belfast sink in the kitchen. One or two houses even had the luxury of a hot water geyser. My house was one of the exceptions in that it had its own toilet fitted in the back bedroom; most of the others, like my neighbours', shared outside toilets. Such conditions were typical for Macclesfield.

Having lived in some comfort in Denmark it felt odd to use outside washing facilities. After I'd been in No. 222 a few days I decided to try for an improvement grant to install a washbasin. The potential demolition order meant that getting a grant was unlikely – but £20 didn't seem much to ask, so my letter was sent to test council reaction. Other residents were eager to see what would happen; they knew that if I could succeed in getting the money then others could apply too.

The application form was filled in and sent off. In January 1972 I got a reply from the town clerk. The answer was 'No', and the letter went on to say that my house had 'an estimated individual life of only five years' and 'was likely to be included in a clearance area under the Housing Acts within ten years in any case.'

Although this reply confirmed what I had already discovered through my solicitor, the logic confused me utterly. My training had taught me that the old had to make way for the new; but my instincts also helped me to recognize a perfectly good building when I saw one. The structure of No. 222 was sound. It had been standing since 1815 and it was now 1972 – almost 160 years.

I decided to make further enquiries about a grant, and thought I might have more success bypassing the Town Clerk's Department and going directly to the Public Health Department. I wanted to know the reason for refusing the grant. Although the council had decided the house only had five years to last, I couldn't see the harm in making a small contribution towards a basin that I could use until demolition.

The first of a flood of letters to the council was drafted at the end of February; it said how disappointed I was with its rather negative attitude. The reply, which arrived a month later, clearly showed that councils suffered from confused thinking. They assumed that if homes lacked a few facilities they were also structurally unsound, and the letter reiterated that because of the property's 'general condition' the house had been placed in 'group one', which 'called for an estimated life to be no more than five years'. Even though subsequent improvement work might have been carried out since the chief medical officer's visit,

> and it may be that a certain amount of modernisation has taken place. . . it is unlikely the basic structure has changed. The statement that the house is likely to be included in a clearance area within ten years is made because a large number of houses within the area are known to be unfit following a recent inspection. And where this is known, the whole area is designated as possible clearance area.

Official vandalism

I was getting nowhere fast. The council clearly wasn't going to agree to a grant, and was still intent on including my house in the future clearance of the area. Local residents had had enough, and decided to join forces to fight back: we formed the Black Road Area Residents' Association, and I was appointed chairman. We were all in the same position: our homes had been labelled blighted property.

The challenge to the council was issued on the grounds that it seemed to be criticizing the structure, rather than the lack of amenities such as washbasins and proper kitchens. I hoped there was a point to be won, and grants to be had, if only we could prove that our properties, having stood for 157 years, could certainly stand for a few more. At the end of June I wrote a letter to the *Macclesfield Express* explaining my case. Its main point was that in housing matters I thought people's feelings were an important consideration. The Black Road residents liked their homes and were prepared to improve them; the last thing anyone wanted was to move into a tower block.

My letter was published in full and caused a commotion. It was the only one printed that week and appeared spread across three columns that took up almost an entire page. One of the main reasons for writing at such length was to draw attention to an exhibition being staged in the town hall of plans to demolish four areas in Macclesfield, one of which was Black Road. I pointed out that, despite the local authority demolition campaign, our properties were in a reasonable condition. The area was also served with good amenities and everybody familiar with it liked the pleasant atmosphere; St George's playing field was used for all sorts of sports, and the Macclesfield Canal was popular with everyone. The letter continued with a warning that all could be lost:

These properties, including my own of 222 Black Road, dating back to between 1812 and 1815. . . are scheduled for demolition in the name of so-called progress, only to be replaced at some later date with new characterless buildings with an expected life normally less than those that they will have replaced.

When I spoke to some of my neighbours in these condemned properties I was struck by their apparent coolness and casual nature.. . . Perhaps this is because they have lived with the problem for at least twenty years, when the council first considered condemning the properties and attaching a five-year life to them. From the early 1950s the houses were considered unfit, having an estimated life in official terms of no more than five years.

The council no doubt enjoys the perpetual condemnation of this area, as among other things it relieves them of their usual responsibilities. I quickly learned of this when I applied for a grant to install a washbasin in my bathroom. When I bought the house in 1971 this was the only basic item missing from the normal list of fixed amenities required for a home. Readers will know that local authorities are obliged to give an owner-occupier half of the cost of providing standard amenities, as long as the property has a minimum official life of fifteen years. I, of course, received a negative reply that will appear familiar to many other interested owners who wish to improve their property.

I said I couldn't accept the refusal of a grant, and wanted to find out the precise reasons for condemning the properties as slums unfit for human habitation when their only apparent disadvantage was old age. My letter continued:

Here therefore we have a perfect example of how easy it is for some official department to condemn an area for fanciful reasons to suit some long-term planning requirement. How can councillors follow this up by withholding normal grants, thus contributing radically to the resultant downfall of a once perfectly good habitable area? This is official vandalism, and the culprit is the Town Hall, especially the Health and Planning departments. How often has this happened before?

A typical history must go something like this: firstly the area is condemned, then the council stops any standard or improvement grants. Residents lose interest in their property and will not pay for the cost of normal improvements as they will suffer financially when the property is demolished. Some leave for other areas, some properties remain unsold, they become dilapidated and vandalized, thus affecting adjacent terrace houses, and so the rot sets in.

The council also has the responsibility of servicing and upkeeping the area. By ignoring this responsibility eyesores develop and decay continues. At this point the local authority can turn round and say that we told you so, this area is unfit for habitation and should be redeveloped.

More people should take note of this official vandalism that is used to justify the posh name of planning. Let us try and put a stop to it now. It's not too late to save these proposed redevelopment areas in Macclesfield. Let us challenge the local authority to return to reality, and let them try to find an alternative based upon the existing fabric. I challenge the official to visit my home and hear if he approves personally of his department's condemnation of what I consider to be a perfectly fit place of habitation. I feel this area can be preserved, thus avoiding ruining the character of an important part of the town. I demand that the council in Macclesfield takes into consideration the viewpoint of the public it is supposed to serve, and avoids the easy pitfall that it is always the right thing to do to jump on the bandwagon of progress without considering the full consequences of such action. When the old buildings have been knocked down and the environment destroyed it will be too late.

I signed that letter as a member of the Royal Institute of British Architects.

Local residents were delighted: they said it was the sort of letter they had wanted to write for years, but were afraid of taking on the council. Until then, therefore, it had always managed to get its own way. Nobody had ever publicly questioned the council's standing or its right to knock down perfectly good houses.

Next we decided to test the level of opinion and see if there were enough people willing to sign a petition supporting the proposal to improve rather than demolish. We demanded that the council take notice of residents' wishes to save their homes, and said that just because the financial committee was short of funds to carry out its programmes it was unfair that homes should be blighted, with no action taken at all. The compulsory purchase order was hanging round our necks like an albatross. Black Road became 'red-lined', which meant that residents were classified a financial risk: it was impossible to get any sort of bank loan or even to hire a television set. Our plight was seen as self-inflicted, when in fact it had been entirely orchestrated by the council.

It tested all our inventiveness to deliver the petition with its eighty signatures, because the Town Clerk's Department refused to receive or discuss it. I was told to put it in the post. But we wanted to make our point and were determined not to be ignored. We decided the only way to make a personal delivery was to mount the petition on a board too big for the post office to accept. At the town hall we were photographed by the local paper. Eventually we were granted an hour-long meeting with the town clerk, where it became obvious that the fight was turning into a battle royal. One or two councillors treated us well, but none said we stood any chance of winning.

But the local response was enormous, and the story appeared on the front page of the *Macclesfield Express*. It was one thing having a letter published, but quite another to make the lead story. The headline declared: 'Council's Policy Official Vandalism'. There had been nothing like it before in Macclesfield. The petition and story proved it wasn't a one-man campaign and that residents, whether owner-occupiers or renting from the council or private landlords, were prepared to join together in the fight. The story struck a chord with hundreds of people who had been in the same position, and letters of support kept appearing in the paper. Encouragement also came from Philip Warburton, the local Methodist minister, and from the Rev. Norman Bingham at St Peter's church.

Muddled thinking

Some farcical mistakes were made. A new buyer, Peter Neal, bought No. 216 with a council mortgage. His repayments were to be made over twenty years for a property that probably wouldn't even be there in five! The council's foolishness at providing a mortgage and then refusing improvement grants was outlined in his letter to the paper at the end of August, in which he wrote:

As the council is supporting me in buying the property I did not really expect any trouble obtaining a standard or improvement grant to bring certain facilities up to standard, including an outside WC that does not work.

But no. In a reply from the town clerk dated 26 July, I was informed the house was not suitable for standard or improvement grants. I have not attempted to try and understand the council's logic, but I am going ahead at my own expense in installing such facilities as I need inside.

I suppose one of the reasons why the house may be cleared within ten years is because it does not have these facilities. I have mentioned that I hope by installing them myself the medical officer of health will look more favourably on the property next time his representatives visit the area. I hope this will lead, along with other properties in the area, to being given a fifteen-year life, thus making the property available for additional improvements, this time in the form of local authority grants. . . . But because of some past decision, now out of date, made by the medical officer of health, my house is not yet eligible.

The letter writers were becoming brave and rebellious. Our story gave people the opportunity to vent their feelings and to criticize the local authority. Older residents sent in colourful descriptions of their recollections of the area's history.

In on the Act

Our local Conservative MP, Nicholas Winterton, came to visit. The *Macclesfield Express* published his letter, in which he appealed to the council to change its mind about demolition – a Tory MP pitting his wits against a Tory council! He wrote:

I hope that Macclesfield Borough Council considers making this an improvement area rather than a redevelopment area, to take advantage of the increased central government improvement grants. The land between Black Road and Smiths Terrace could be used for extension of properties, and these cottages could be brought up to date with modern kitchens, bathrooms and WCs.

This could be a pleasant residential area. I've seen some extremely nice cottages which are a picture. It would be a tragedy to break up the community by demolishing the houses.

We have seen evidence of areas which have been cleared and have just become stagnant with nothing on them, the community dispersed. These people want to spend money to improve their homes which are basically strong and well constructed. They have spent money on them and they could be improved even more if improvement grants were made available.

The great advantage that Nicholas Winterton had over the council was that he had obviously read the 1969 Housing Act. This piece of legislation turned out to be our best friend. It was designed to promote refurbishment and halt the expensive and ailing post-war housing programme by stopping demolition. Although the Act had been passed three years previously, it hadn't registered in Macclesfield.

On closer examination of the small print we discovered it was possible for us to prepare a report on our area, recommending it for regeneration. The Act went to great lengths to explain that the document should be the work of qualified persons with local knowledge. It was the first piece of government policy to attempt to acknowledge ordinary people and make them responsible for their own locality. This was too good an opportunity to miss. With the help of residents and Chris Hogben, a surveyor friend, I prepared a lengthy report.

Hogben and I had met at Manchester University during the

campaign to save areas of old housing in the city at Withington, Ladybarn, Moss Side and Didsbury. They were all threatened by slum clearance ordered by the city council's notorious Alf Young. We had prepared surveys on the condition of homes which were then presented to public inquiries by residents challenging demolition orders, so this was no new task we had set ourselves.

A deafening report

Painstakingly we spelled out our case. Residents were united in the aim to save and improve homes, we said. We wanted to give the properties an extended life of at least thirty years, and new government legislation was there to help us. We compiled a complete social survey of the residents, how they felt, which houses were occupied and which were empty, the financial viability of our plans and the benefits of the area – how it was a convenient location with plenty of amenities. It was copiously illustrated with photographs, showing that the properties were potential gems.

The key to saving our homes lay in securing a General Improvement Area declaration. GIAs had been introduced by the 1969 Housing Act to identify areas where demolition could not take place and where renovation work would be helped by central government grants for play areas, car parking, landscaping and so on. Additional improvement grants could be made available for new bathrooms, improved electric wiring, new roofing and damp proofing, new windows and central heating. At that time Maccles- field had no GIAs. There were no precedents, then, but to be declared a GIA was crucial to us. There would have been no point in tackling the problem piecemeal – everything had to be improved.

To our dismay the council appeared to know virtually nothing of the current legislation. Included with our report was a resumé of the relevant sections of the '69 Act and a selected list of circulars to read. If Black Road was to stand any chance of becoming a General Improvement Area it was obvious we would have to educate the council, step by step.

Circular 65/69 of the 1969 Act was of special significance because it recognized the importance of residents' commitment. It suggested that council officials should visit areas under consideration to see for themselves where people were most likely to welcome and undertake an improvement scheme. It also stated that the local authority should make every effort to gain the confidence of residents and owners so as to secure their co-operation.

One of the aims of the report was to convince the council of our scheme's financial viability, and so information was also provided to explain the Housing Act and subsequent government circulars. This included, for instance, the fact that local authority contributions to owner-occupiers' improvement and repair costs in certain parts of England, including Macclesfield, had increased from half to three-quarters, up to a limit of £2000. That sort of change could have been our make or break, because we needed as much money as possible.

Elderly and very poor people could easily be included in the scheme with the help of local authority maturity loans. These worked on the basis that people might not be able to pay back the principal borrowed until a 'special event' – such as on their death through their estate, or on the sale of the property. Interest only was paid in the interim. The scheme was particularly important for owners who would qualify for a grant but could not afford their part of the deal. For every £1500 of grant they were expected to raise £500; the Department of Health and Social Security was obliged to pay the interest on the loan for the very poor.

To show our commitment we explained that the Black Road Area Residents' Association was already formed and had an action group to act as the liaison team. The team's function was to represent residents and others in the area, and to negotiate closely with the local authority to ensure that a satisfactory result was achieved. Then I went to great lengths to detail the physical condition of the properties. With the help of Chris Hogben and Bob Young, a public health officer, I surveyed each home to identify the extent of work needed.

In one house stone steps were uneven, in another the stairs were very steep and the chimneys were unsafe – if you lit a fire in one flue the smoke came out of all four chimneypots. Some houses let in the rain – there were areas of penetrating and driving damp, and some rising damp. Several doors were only about 5 feet 6 inches high. Most houses lacked toilets, washbasins and proper kitchens, and there was generally a bad arrangement of space. Electric wiring was in poor condition and timber was rotting – many timber gutters hadn't been repaired since they were first put in place in 1815.

Then came the list of environmental improvements. Residents needed easy access to the backs of their homes, which at the time of the survey were dingy. People had fallen over on their way to the outside toilets because there was no lighting.

Finally we had to cost the work needed to bring each property up to scratch. The value of each home was around £1100, and the cost to renovate one between £1672 and £2819. (In the late eighties they were worth at least £40,000.) We showed that the cost of repairs and improvements came within the budget limitations laid down in the 1969 Housing Act.

The report's conclusion stated:

In the introduction . . . we referred to the considerations which are the central criteria for making the area one of improvement. Our surveyors have shown that in their professional opinion they feel that the properties are generally in good condition, and this is borne out by the low cost of repairs referred to in our report.

By organizing their support the people of the area have shown their solid interest in making the area an improvement

THE BADDIES

Above: Alison & Peter Smithson

Above: Ernö Goldfinger

Above: Le Corbusier

Left and right: Hugh Wilson & Lewis Womersley

BETTER BY DESIGN

Above: Guggenheim Mu
New York: pretty good a

Left: Swan Theatre, Stra
upon-Avon: coup de théâ

Right: Refuge Building,
Manchester: restored to
perfection

Below: Uplands Conference
Centre: talking point

THE GOODIES

Above left: Thomas Telford. *Above right*: Renzo Piano.
Bottom left: Lord Scarman. *Bottom right*: Edward Cullinan

THE Mirror

FORWARD WITH BRITAIN

ober 24, 1985   18p

Britain needs action

MY FEARS FOR THE FUTURI

by Prince Charles

C E CHARLES'S fears for the of life in Britain vealed yesterday.

reses a nation of reas and inner-city on unless action is w.

rince's feelings were to his architect friend kney in secret talks on al train in the West on Monday. Mr said:

very worried that when comes King there will areas in the inner cities e minorities will be

Divided

nts to stop a divided nd wants the Governnd professional people servants, economists, and surveyors to e problems and not let er.

nts the poor in inner have access to the ple so that they can mselves.

ows there is no quick but he knows that

HACKNEY: Train meeting

By EDWARD VALE & TED OLIVER

something must be done soon—that the time is ripe.

The Prince has many friends in high places and I am sure they will do their utmost to find a solution.

He clearly does not want a nation of haves and have-nots. He is not asking for the world. He just wants opportunities for under-privileged people.

Royal adviser reveals Prince's secret thoughts

The Prince is very worried. He is particularly concerned that racial minorities are becoming alienated.

Last night there was confusion about what the Prince had said to Macclesfield-based Mr Hackney.

Yes, Buckingham Palace agreed. Charles DID have discussions with the architect about the problems of the inner cities. And he was deeply concerned.

But the Palace said the talks were private, and added : "We

regard Mr Hackney's words as a paraphrase. In no way would the Prince of Wales use terms like those quoted.

But the spokesman confirmed that Charles was aware of what Mr Hackney had said. And would not be issuing a denial.

Mr Hackney, vice-president of the International Union of Architects, with members in 96 countries, insisted that he had reported the Prince correctly

Turn to Page Two

CHARLES: No-go worry

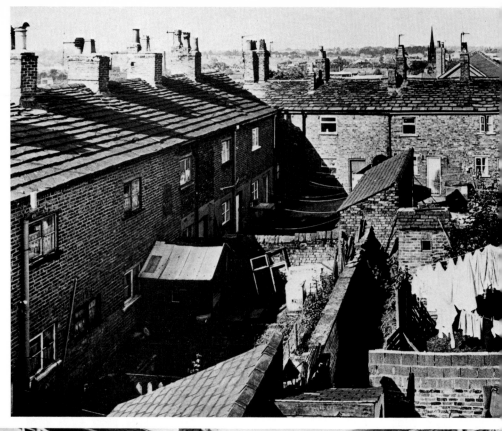

CK ROAD NO. 2

ve left: Courtyard before work
an

ve right: Demolishing the toilets

t: The end of the road is at hand

The way it was

Above: The way ahead, Hawes Street

Below: Homeless

area, thus providing themselves with a long-term security, knowing their homes are safe for at least thirty years.

The report, which ran to fifty-four pages and was subsidized by money and professional assistance from local residents and well-wishers, was circulated to every councillor. Then we waited. And waited.

Fearing the council's silence, I then produced a supplementary report in September, two months after the first. It compared the cost of completing our scheme with that of knocking houses down, and really brought the message home.

We have decided to add a general statement considering the overall cost of house improvement as compared with total demolition. Total cost of improving the thirty-three dwellings would cost £74,250, our way.

If one compares this with the total cost to replace thirty-three dwellings with new buildings one can get an idea of the saving involved. Taking the figures we have in our preliminary report dated 28 July 1972, we quoted a figure of £6600 for the total cost of a new dwelling, with land acquisitions, construction and services. This gives a total replacement cost of £207,800.

Our figures highlighted the terrible waste of the previous decades. Many millions of pounds could have been saved if renovation had been the fashion.

In addition to the fact that the scheme to keep Black Road cost a third of the work planned by the council, we would also be saving it money in another way. If the local authority went ahead with its scheme it would have to find the entire £207,800. And worse still, it might have to borrow the money from central government to be repaid over sixty years – making the final cost, with interest, well over £1 million. By encouraging residents in a self-help scheme a small portion of the costs would be provided in grants – £1500 for each of the thirty-three homes – and the rest would be provided by the residents themselves. At the end of the day the local authority might be finding £45,000 for improvement grants, part of which could be borrowed as a subsidy from central government, compared with £207,800 where it would have to borrow the lot. There was simply no cost comparison.

Still we waited. Every time I called the council I was told everyone was busy and that Black Road residents couldn't expect to push to the front of the queue. Council officers assured me that the report would be considered, and that preliminary steps had been made to check out my qualifications.

Finally impatience got the better of me and I took the report to Peter Walker, Secretary of State for the Environment; I informed the council that we had gone over their heads and were seeking encouragement from the minister. But still there was delay, and so to raise our spirits we started the 'Keep It Up, Black Road' campaign.

We were in the news again, and more letters were sent to the local paper. People jumped at the chance to voice opinions which were clearly at odds with council policies. Complete strangers wrote to say that the preservation of terrace homes was important, and, despite local authority slum declarations, they were actually good for people's health because they were familiar and cosy. Local architects joined the debate and one, Harry Ward, stressed how necessary it was to preserve people's individuality, which would only be possible if the Black Road homes were saved. 'The Black Road Action Group deserves our gratitude and neighbourly support for this enterprise,' he wrote to the papers. 'May we hope not only that the council will set the necessary machinery in motion, but will do its best to ensure that the pace of action is maintained.' We had already had the support of our local Tory MP. Now Len Walton, leader of the local Labour Party, wrote asking: 'Where does democracy begin and end?'

Soon our story spread further afield. On 5 October 1972 the *Manchester Evening News* wrote about us, and this was followed by a report in the *Guardian*. Appearing under the simple headline

'Scheme to Save Homes', the piece was only brief; nevertheless national coverage of any kind was a great morale-booster.

The light at the end of the tunnel

At last, after months of waiting, our report was examined by the council and achieved the unusual distinction of winning all-party support. The first hurdle seemed to be over, and on 12 October the *Macclesfield Express* ran an editorial congratulating us:

It was indeed refreshing to hear praise for the case put forward by the Black Road Area Action Group from all sides of the chamber at last week's meeting at Macclesfield Town Council. There are many who feel that Macclesfield has already lost too much cottage property, which, with a little foresight, might well have been saved to the benefit and character of the borough and the town's finances. The Black Road people are to be congratulated on the way they have gone about their 'save our homes' campaign. They have not merely dug their heels in the ground and said to the council you cannot pull our homes down, but have with considerable skill put forward a case to show why and how cheap it would be to make Black Road an improvement area as against a clearance area.

They have tried, and have succeeded, in co-operating with the corporation. This is why they deserve all the compliments which came from all parties.

Many of these town cottages, the majority of which are terraced, have been made into homes which are a credit to their owners . . . and let us not forget that when we talk about houses we are talking about people's homes.

It is unusual indeed for all sections of the council to be in agreement, but this is the one subject on which they are.

The council's next move was to instruct the Public Health Department to look at our proposals in detail and come back with recommendations, but the cloak of secrecy drawn over the proceedings was worrying. Residents felt excluded and asked to join in. It was unlikely that the council would agree to sit down with residents' groups, because previous meetings with groups other than ours had degenerated into shouting matches. But we wanted to take part, and needed the council to be aware of our enthusiasm.

I sent the paper another letter, which again appeared in full. Diplomacy was required. We wanted to set a precedent of negotiation, and used the opportunity to promise we would be on our best behaviour:

> The courtesy and civility shown so far in our campaign will be carried through in any direct negotiations with the council and council officers. This we guarantee. After all, it is for our own benefit as well as the corporation's. We throw out this challenge. If accepted, we feel a new landmark will have been achieved in the area of public participation and local government. A landmark that may go down as the turning point in the tide against what many observers see as the growing trend of public apathy, a trend that will eventually prove dangerous in our democratic system unless it is terminated. We in the Black Road area can contribute here. We ask that we be given the chance.

Across the table

To our surprise we were invited to talk to councillors and officers. First a special preliminary meeting was held to consider the implications. Officials were worried that if we were given the privilege of speaking in council then everybody in the town would want to do the same. They also thought we might be breaking standing orders or be seen as receiving preference over others.

Eventually they decided they would sit down with us. The event was a mould-breaker, an example of real democracy, and it excited the press. 'Democracy in action is a stirring sight,' cried the *Macclesfield Advertiser*.

We have seen an example of how democracy has proved it's not merely an ideal but a workable and effective tool.. . . here is a group of people who know far better than anyone else the circumstances of their environment, and the newly released housing strategy report.

We would suggest in future the setting up of street committees to discuss the best way to make the necessary improvements.

Public participation may be a hackneyed phrase, but it is undeniable proof that, where practical, it is a highly desirable feature of government today.

Following our meeting, the carefully worded council report conceded that there was 'potential' for improvement areas in the town. It also indicated that such improvement could provide a new way of looking at the future of around 1200 local properties affected by clearance plans. It went on to mention our call for a GIA at Black Road. There were reservations about the age of the properties, and technical reasons were given for why our homes might not qualify for improvement – they were still saying they were in poor condition, and there were too many of them. The council knew there would be less risk involved in renovating another area where the houses were in better shape. However, our determination had been made clear and the council noted that the one saving grace for Black Road was the enthusiasm of local residents.

A special committee was set up jointly by the Housing and Planning departments. Discussions began. By the beginning of

November we felt we were making progress. There was no GIA declaration, the homes hadn't yet been saved, but the talking had started – so we issued an optimistic statement saying we were halfway there.

Resident buyout

The next chink in the armour was a letter from the Town Clerk and Chief Executive, David Hargreaves, who had just taken over after Walter Isaac retired. It was couched in the usual formal council jargon, but declared that Black Road was officially being considered as a 'potential' GIA. The council still hadn't made any firm commitment.

The waiting was agony but we had to be patient. Any displays of anger or frustration would have jeopardized our chances. And so, continuing our policy of tact and diplomacy, we disguised our disappointment at the council's use of the word 'potential' for our improvement area and wrote to the *Macclesfield Express*:

> We are indeed pleased that our efforts in spring this year have been rewarded with what we consider a vote of confidence in the proposals we have advocated. At the last meeting of the Black Road Area Action Committee, it was confirmed that three area officers . . . would form a working committee to negotiate with the officers of the local authority in all matters. They represent a general cross-section of the type of work inherent in the improvement proposals, and all live in an area now considered potential to an improvement area.

The press was still following our story, and the *Daily Mail* appeared on the scene at the end of November with a hard-hitting piece which landed me in hot water because as an architect I had dared to speak out against my colleagues. It was considered a terrible crime, for which I was reported to the professional body.

Architect Rod Hackney, 30, the campaign leader, said: 'We have avoided a scheme that would have been quite simply official vandalism. The cottages have stood for so long, and, professionally, I am convinced that after improvements they will be good for another 100 years at least. I feel that too many of my fellow architects are only concerned with knocking buildings down and creating their own fancies without any regard for what people actually want.'

My comments upset several local architects, who felt that I was already behaving in a cavalier fashion and shouldn't be living in the area where I was working. There were then quite rigid codes of conduct preventing architects from advertising or touting for work.

The *Daily Mail* piece was completely misinterpreted. I was simply trying to say that the policy of building new wasn't always the answer to housing problems. My argument wasn't made on the basis of old versus new; I was saying that people should be allowed to stay where they were happy and should be given every encouragement to improve old houses to a reasonable standard. The fuss blew over.

There had been enough talking, and residents wanted to see some action. So we set to work helping tenants buy their homes. There was a strong possibility that, once the blight was lifted and the scheme was underway, property prices would rocket beyond most people's pockets. It was therefore important for them to buy early.

A number of properties were owned by a landlady living in Colwyn Bay in North Wales. She was retired and couldn't afford the upkeep on her houses because she was as poor as the tenants. A package deal was devised through which a group of tenants offered £1600 for their five homes. It was not a great deal of money, but the landlady was pleased because receiving a lump sum was more useful to her than the rent, which, at around twelve shillings a week, barely covered the estate agent's charge to collect it. Other similar buy-outs followed. Just one resident didn't buy – he elected to remain a local authority tenant having decided he was too old to become an owner-occupier. This meant that the local council was unavoidably involved in the scheme, because it too was responsible for the upkeep of a house.

The year of action

The weeks were flicking past and still there was no news about the GIA. But time was of the essence. Building costs were rising at an alarming rate – 30 per cent inflation in 1972, with similar predictions for 1973. We faced the prospect of being unable to afford the proposals, and needed the GIA declaration urgently before costs spiralled too high.

The festive season came and went. We designed our own Christmas cards, using a collage of all the best headlines, and sent them to supporters. The holiday period was also used for organizing parties and creating the right mood for 1973 as the year of action. It was to be a very important year.

A string of journalists visited Black Road and our story cropped up all over the place during the winter and spring. We were featured in magazines and newspapers, then on radio and TV. The local press, particularly, remained a great encouragement to us. At the end of January the *Macclesfield Advertiser* stopped our spirits flagging by congratulating us on the campaign to date:

It has provided an object lesson in public relations with Macclesfield corporation, and has helped enormously to break down the natural barriers between local government and local people. The man from the council is all too often an ogre, someone to be regarded with suspicion. Now that the Black Road campaign has all but succeeded, and everybody knows just how it's succeeded, it can be readily seen how public participation in such a scheme can have enormous beneficial effects.

In future years there will be many Black Roads springing up in the news in Macclesfield as the town tries to improve itself. We hope that the lessons learned recently won't be forgotten.

Eventually, on 22 March, news of the General Improvement Area declaration was leaked a couple of weeks before the official announcement date. Against the odds, we had saved our homes and won a major battle.

Showing off

A show house was needed, to give inspiration and demonstrate just how dramatic the changes could be. I had already started work on my own place and so, after I had moved temporarily to our site office at 214 Black Road, the job was completed as swiftly as possible. It took around three months and involved replacing or restoring virtually everything apart from the roof, which was to be repaired in one go with the others along the terrace. I had to knock down walls, replace the chimney, fit new windows, put new stairs in the front room, enlarge the kitchen, install a bathroom, replace the electrical wiring, replumb the entire house, carry out damp proofing, replaster, lay new floors and decorate each room.

On 13 September 1973 the task was finished. It had cost exactly what the report had stated, but I had to spend something like 1500 hours of my own time on it to keep within the budget. The building industry had seen a dramatic 60 per cent price rise, and that's what was to turn Black Road into a major self-help scheme. Because of tight budgets, residents ended up doing the very things they thought they would have to pay builders for. Rising costs meant we simply couldn't afford the rates builders charge.

An open day was held to celebrate the completion of No. 222. It was attended by members of the public and all the local dignitaries – councillors, the mayor and Nicholas Winterton, MP. The day was a huge success, with everyone patting everyone else on the back. I had brought in an Arne Jacobsen-designed table and chairs which took pride of place in the kitchen, and the washbasin which had started the whole saga was sparkling in the bathroom. The work on my house had finally demonstrated that the project was not a far-fetched fantasy.

Community at work

I became the architect for the scheme, and we all had to work fast towards the deadline of June 1974 when new legislation was being introduced to cut grants. It was a far from smooth ride, with plenty of obstacles to overcome – personality clashes, delays in getting materials and people making mistakes.

The work started with the demolition of the old outside toilets and washhouses. By this time most homes had had their own basins and lavatories installed, and so the buildings were redundant. Knocking down the hated sheds provided a good, therapeutic start, and everyone joined in. Some of the men in the road were already skilled labourers or were good at DIY, and so they were able to carry out their own repairs. Others learned by watching or by trial and error, and I was on call the whole time to offer advice and help. The women, too, were far from being bystanders. One, married to a builder, saw him plastering and then, much to his surprise and maybe hers, picked up the trowel and finished the job.

Team spirit grew as the weeks passed and people swopped skills – an electrician would offer to help with rewiring a neighbour's house in exchange for assistance with his own central heating, and so on. No one was left out. Pensioners were aided by their families and friends, and kept the entire workforce supplied with endless cups of tea and biscuits. During the year-long improvement period the residents put in an estimated sixty thousand hours of labour.

The trade press picked up the story, and in May *Building Design* ran a large feature discussing the implications of our pioneering residents' scheme for local councils and criticizing their defunct systems. It also highlighted the benefit of having an architect on site, living and working there to oversee and assist residents. Black Road was described as a 'spanner in the works of Manchester's magnificent flying slum clearance machine'.

Repeat performances of Rod Hackney's Black Road show are pencilled in for Manchester and Birmingham. The lessons are clear, although the aggro and the organization operation is more than any one normal human being could cope with. Self-help improvement under GIA is cheaper, more effective and environmentally less polluting than the simplistic expensive local authority clearance renewal programmes. The architecture involved is by no means a fine art. Self-help building construction, running in conjunction with small unit contractors, makes a mockery out of professional expertise in the residential sector.

Although the full implications might not be quite clear yet, when the dust has settled around the Black Road site, when all the residents have finished laying their carpets, and when the case has been made, it will be apparent that Rod Hackney's scheme was at least an applicable noise in an ill-conceived system. Bye-laws will have been meaningfully bypassed, impenetrable legal knots will have been loosened. The militant community will have appreciated the extent of its power. The residents of Smiths Terrace and Black Road have become bona fide maintenance builders with a real understanding of how houses get built. The patchwork brickwork will have weathered itself into the rest of Macclesfield, and the next performance will run just a little bit more smoothly.

In Black Road the motto is small is beautiful. Participants, from pensioners to unmarried mothers, are happy, the contractors are happy, Rod Hackney is happy and Macclesfield is happy.

Television crews became a part of everyday life, but because Macclesfield hadn't previously featured in the media there were a few problems. Councillors in particular were used to running the town and didn't like to be left out. One Granada programme really stirred things up by concentrating solely on residents. There were still some sensitive feelings to be bruised. Two further programmes followed. One, *Help Yourself to a House*, was an entire documentary on our work. It was a superb piece of production by Ramsay Short, an architect and great friend to the project. The second programme was all about self-help around the country. We were transformed from a group of battered residents fighting for survival to minor celebrities. The story had made us a curiosity and a tourist attraction. Busloads of people turned up to have a look at what we had done. Our only regret was not having built outside toilets for the visitors.

The road to success

By the end of 1974 work on all thirty-three homes was complete. The mayor planted a ceremonial tree and unveiled a plaque – the first of many commemorating such projects. There is always a big fuss about the plaque, which probably causes more problems than any other part of the scheme. Should the wording read 'His Worship the Mayor' or 'The Worshipful Mayor'? What colour should the velvet curtain be? In any event, the details have to be decided with great care to ensure everyone is satisfied.

We had to pay for both the plaque and the tree because environmental works were part of a trust deed. There were special legal arrangements, which included being granted a zero rating from the district valuer. This allowed us to control the upkeep of outside areas: we became the first residents in the country to collect our own rates, which we spent on maintaining the car parking spaces and the road inside the scheme, lighting, landscaping and snow clearance.

Politically, Black Road was a great success. The residents were praised by politicians of all complexions. The Socialists considered it a great victory for the working man, with residents all pulling together in a co-operative effort, while the Tories saw it as a great victory for those who helped themselves. The *Macclesfield Advertiser* marked the final celebrations by pointing out that all the ingredients were a success: 'Let us hope that what has happened can be used as an example to us, not just in Macclesfield, but other towns who've sent their representatives to look at just how Macclesfield has worked.' The *Macclesfield Express* echoed these sentiments: 'Now the idea may go to Belfast where authorities feel similar schemes could help the case to ease community conflict. It would be nice indeed if Macclesfield's ideas went a little way to calming the troubled waters.'

The real story was the triumph of the people. The scheme had boosted their morale and self-respect as well as giving them the responsibility of a mortgage. There had been 18 per cent unemployment in the area before work began; by the time it was completed many of the previously unemployed were able to use their newly acquired skills to set up their own businesses or find jobs – a feat which would have been impossible without the personal confidence acquired through the self-help scheme.

Everyone wanted to know how we had won. I was asked to talk at conferences all over the country, and gradually our ideas spread. I was invited to work at Northenden in Manchester, in the Woodvale area of Belfast, at George Arthur Road, Birmingham, at Clitheroe in Lancashire, at Cleator Moor and Carlisle in Cumbria, in Leicester, Derby and many other places. The interest was so great that I couldn't handle all the work and began to employ other people. My business took off and offices were set up at each scheme. The only way to make these projects really work was to have an architect living and working on-site twenty-four hours a day, and that became a condition of contract for all the architects I employed.

Black Road Number 2, a quarter of a mile up the road from the first scheme, was started in 1975 and completed four years later. Its success proved that the idea could be repeated and was therefore more than just a one-off scheme. Nevertheless it took some years for the Black Road project to be recognized as an architectural scheme, particularly by the profession itself. Most contemporary architects were either scornful or bemused. If there wasn't a style, how could it be called architecture? They preferred to see it as the work of a builder rather than that of an architect.

It was the kind of attitude that showed how far the Modernist principle had departed from the concept of building for people. Community architects (the label was coined by Charles Knevitt in a *Building Design* article of July 1975, after a visit to Black Road Number 2) were seen as fringe activists. We were rebels, and we were letting the side down by dabbling in folksy nonsense. However, as projects were set up around Britain the successes made themselves noticed. And in November 1975 Michael Hook, writing about Black Road in the *Architects Journal*, analyzed for the first time what the community approach meant to the professional and how it had challenged and altered accepted rules and ideas:

> The scheme's failure or success could so easily have floundered on the tide of pedantic rule-worshipping. However, the declared commitment of the elected representatives, combined with the permanent presence of the architect on site supported by the chairman of the trust who was a qualified clerk of works, had done much to encourage the relaxed interpretation of so many regulations.
>
> Standards of privacy were not enforced, neighbours them-

selves agreed to accept being overlooked; relaxed standards were accepted for kerbs and turning circles; car parking space was limited for only those households with cars, with an additional three spaces for visitors.

Among the controls eased were public health and bye-law controls. Communal soil pipes and shared incoming water supply were accepted. Economy of planning often produced door widths, ceiling heights and staircases below normal minimum standards. Steep staircases were retained where replacement to modern standards would have demanded more expense and replanning; party walls were 4.5 inches; brickwork was retained. But all houses were improved to a minimum twelve-point standard required for grants.

The article endorsed the usefulness of architects in renovating properties. It helped to show, too, that there was a place for professionals with a broad outlook. Architects were not simply building designers but could perform a variety of functions – as planners; as directors of national agencies, local authorities, government design departments and property development committees; and as community organizers. The single-minded specialist approach of the Modernist school was shown to be just one of many ways for architects to practice. This new understanding of our potential role had taken several years to gather momentum, but suddenly the media everywhere wanted to know what the community approach was. I was invited to conferences around the world, and in Australia I made the front page of several newspapers as 'The Man Who Went to War over a Washbasin'.

Meanwhile work on my PhD, which had led me to buy 222 Black Road in the first place, had been shelved. It was not until 1979 that I managed to complete it.

5 The Wasteland

In sharp contrast to the vibrancy, idealism and, often misguided, optimism of the previous decade, the seventies saw Britain plunge into a period of political and economic stagnation. It was a time of disillusionment, when the country was made sharply aware that it was no longer a great world power, and that post-war promises of a brighter future still remained unfulfilled. The boom of the sixties had ground to a halt. Reduction of loans from the International Monetary Fund (because Britain was heavily in debt) precipitated an economic decline which was compounded by a period of world recession, the oil crisis and the three-day week.

Jobs and houses were the two major concerns of most ordinary people. Unemployment was rising dramatically with the closure of mills and factories, new and hurriedly built housing estates were falling into disrepair because local councils couldn't keep pace with maintenance, and yet at the same time old street communities were still being threatened with demolition. Despite any early lessons which may have been learned by the saving of Black Road, councils around the country were still determined to pursue costly building programmes, and so continued to spawn a dependency culture: more and more people were having to depend on the state, rather than themselves, for survival.

Additional pressure to keep the construction machine rolling had been brought to bear when Britain joined the European Economic Community (EEC) in 1973. The government became acutely aware of our image abroad when comparisons were made between member states concerning productivity, modernization in industry, and living conditions. Both central government and local authorities were anxious to make a good impression, and so looked to the construction industry to help in the latest drive to inject new life into town and city centres and to generate an atmosphere of prosperity in which living standards could be improved.

If only politicians had taken the trouble to listen to the gossip in shops and pubs, they might have learned some valuable lessons from the people on the receiving end of their policies. They would have heard first-hand accounts – that estates were unpopular, that councils were slow at carrying out the ever-increasing numbers of repairs, that people didn't want to be resettled into homes which were clearly council-owned, and that for all their faults the so-called 'slums' were preferred to the towers.

The numbers game

Shortly after joining the EEC the government proudly announced that there were some 344 dwellings for every thousand people, a figure which compared favourably with the 346 in the Common Market as a whole. There were also boasts that 80 per cent of British homes had bathrooms, compared with only 68 per cent in West Germany and 41 per cent in France. The UK could also rejoice in more flush toilets per capita than elsewhere in the Community.

The figures were typical examples of political rhetoric and had little practical significance. France, for example, has a large rural community where amenities are usually of a lower standard than those in urban areas. A typical farmhouse with low doorways, rickety stairs and an outside privy is considered adequate and even quaint. Nationwide figures would therefore have different implications when compared to Britain, where the majority of the population lives in urban areas. In a city those conditions would be unacceptable and the house declared unfit for human habitation.

Government announcements were a limp attempt to gloss over the real problems of the decaying inner city environment. It would have been a real jolt to the system if statistics on overcrowding and homelessness had been exposed and real comparisons made with similar cities in Holland, Germany and Denmark, rather than the southern rural areas of Italy and Spain.

Bringing the house down

Public anxiety about housing was to be reinforced by the partial destruction of the Pruitt Igoe estate in St Louis, in the USA. It was a different story from Ronan Point because architectural collapse was preceded by social collapse, which resulted in *deliberate* demolition of housing blocks. A portion of the estate was blown up right at the start of the Black Road battle in 1972, and boosted our determination to fight against council towers. I clearly remember the dramatic newspaper pictures of collapsing towers engulfed in clouds of dust and rubble, and I recall reading that in America the event had been televised nationwide because of strong public feeling against these buildings.

Constructed only seventeen years before, in 1953, the thirty-three identical, eleven-storey blocks of 2800 apartments designed by Minoru Yamasaki had been held up as an award-winning example of the revolutionary new Modernist style. However, the building work had been hurried and shoddy. Massive cost cuts had been made. Structural and technical problems soon showed themselves, and even at the official opening ceremony there were problems with broken lifts. The catalogue of technical failures grew week by week – windows refused to open, glass panes fell out, fixtures and fittings were constantly breaking.

The Pruitt estate was built when St Louis was still a segregated city, and the blocks were occupied entirely by blacks. However, when desegregation was introduced an unsuccessful attempt was made to integrate whites into the buildings. Neglect, vandalism and decay drove many people to leave, and by the early seventies 65 per cent of the flats were empty. In 1972 the Department of Housing and Urban Development, which had originally commissioned the building, decided to demolish the three central towers.

Planners and architects in St Louis believed the problem was purely a social one and thought that, by thinning out the blocks and reducing the population, the estate could be more easily controlled. However, time proved them wrong. Structural and technical faults increased in conjunction with crime and social problems, and by 1980 all thirty-three towers had been razed to the ground.

The story captured press headlines on both sides of the Atlantic, and it sparked off a new round of debate in Britain. Architects here supported their American colleagues, refusing to acknowledge that the design and planning of the estate were at fault. The extensive problems were blamed on bad management and abuse by tenants.

There was, however, one important social study to emerge at this time: *Defensible Space*, by an American named Oscar Newman. In his book Newman pinpointed design as a major fault in public housing, and called for changes in the way estates were built so as to reduce the common sense of alienation. He identified the vast open spaces around towers and the communal halls, passages and stairs as major factors contributing to the creation of a hostile environment. Newman suggested that the spaces should be divided up and that the responsibility for their upkeep should be handed over to residents. These ideas had, of course, been successfully put into practice in the Black Road scheme, where residents willingly took control of public areas and guarded them enthusiastically. If a passer-by dropped a piece of litter someone would see him and hand it back.

Up until the Pruitt Igoe demolition people living in British estates had felt condemned to a life sentence – but now they were shown an alternative. A number of local authorities took drastic action and blew up their most troublesome towers. To some extent this was just a public relations exercise, to demonstrate that councils cared about their tenants and were prepared to listen to their complaints. Most tenants leaving the towers were rehoused in low-rise council houses.

Political failure

The demolitions solved nothing. Indeed, the financial problems facing councils were exacerbated. They were still expected to repay the government loans taken out to build the towers, but demolition had cut off their rent income.

During the see-sawing between Labour and Conservative administrations in these years government departments were in a state of panic – the coffers were empty. Nothing was left to repair the damage. But there was no public admission of failure.

Legislation such as the 1969 Housing Act was intended to reverse the slum clearance policy and encourage refurbishment of existing buildings. But the effects had been minimal. In 1974 the Conservative government under Edward Heath passed a new Housing Act. Drawing on the 1969 Act, the latest legislation further encouraged the rehabilitation of pre-1919 properties. The government was fully aware that public housing programmes were becoming prohibitively costly, and hoped that by sponsoring the repair of old buildings the burden of the state's responsibility to build could be alleviated.

In addition to the General Improvement Areas of 1969, the 1974 Act introduced Housing Action Areas (HAAs), which could be designated so as to make grants available for restoring homes in very poor condition. Where a GIA demanded that properties had to be renovated to provide a minimum thirty-year life extension, standards here were relaxed and money was made available for more short-term improvements.

The Conservative government also made it clear that it mistrusted the ability of local authorities to act as efficient housing managers. The setting up of housing associations was encouraged through the revamping and restructuring of the Housing Corporation, which received a direct grant from government that was then passed on to approved, registered housing associations. It set the standards for these bodies and had the power to close down any that fell below par.

With assistance from the Housing Corporation over three thousand of these independently run associations and societies were formed and helped to dismantle local authority control. They took over the management of many council properties and funded new building projects. The idea had some merit, because associations often controlled small numbers of houses, around two or three hundred, and so were able to offer a better service than the councils with their leviathan stocks. However, although these properties were intended to become a 'third arm' – the others being private and council-owned homes – their expansion was prevented by cutbacks during the latter part of the decade.

Saving Saltley

I had learned a great deal in Macclesfield, but as I began to tackle other work it became clear there was no such thing as a set approach to community architecture. Success lay in recognizing the idiosyncrasies of areas, in understanding the people and in learning about the various ways in which local councils worked.

The 1974 Act offered a great boost to the new community approach and was perfectly timed to help in my next venture, at George Arthur Road in the Saltley district of Birmingham. After witnessing the results of Birmingham City Council's demolition derby, the residents had banded together in an attempt to stop plans for high-rise development in their area.

Saltley, two miles from the city centre and best known for its massive gasworks, had originally been considered by the council as a prime target for new estates. The residents had other ideas, and wrote to me in 1974 after watching a television programme based on my work. My first response was to invite the group to Macclesfield so they could see the results at Black Road and talk to the residents. Impressed, they decided to launch their own campaign by issuing a direct challenge to Birmingham City Council. Officials were invited to look at the alternative of saving homes in place of demolition.

Opening doors

The Saltley group also persuaded the local Community Development Project, set up by the Home Office to pay for professional community advisers, to employ me on a trial basis. My task was to prepare proposals showing that the houses, although old, had the potential to be renovated and brought up to modern standards; with that confirmation the residents would be able to challenge the council's plans.

I shared an office with the CDP and managed to highlight the residents' case by making a TV programme, *Open Door*. Filming was fun, but more importantly it uncovered the area's history and encouraged residents to be proud of their neighbourhood and work together. Publicity is a vital weapon in community schemes. People threatened with losing their homes always make good copy, and battles against bureaucracy will continue to be potent issues. Journalists were becoming increasingly aware of the housing debate, and, after years of acting as part of the political propaganda machine by praising new blocks as being 'airy', 'clean' and 'warm', they had begun to listen to tenants. Architects were also coming under fire for producing poor designs – not just for housing but for offices, shopping complexes, schools and hospitals.

Open Door was the catalyst. One of the most effective scenes in the programme showed residents simply standing outside their front doors as the mobile camera moved from one end of the long street to the other. It said more than any commentary could about how proud the people were of their homes and their street. It also demonstrated how well the mix of ages and races worked.

But despite all the publicity the George Arthur Road Group had its work cut out. Not only was there a battle with the council's apparently intransigent Environmental Health and Urban Renewal Departments, it also faced problems acquiring property leases. These documents were held by London, City and Westcliff, a large company and a subsidiary of the giant Lonrho. Once the leases expired, which was imminent, the properties would revert by law to the freeholder. Residents were threatened with losing their homes in two ways – either to the council bulldozers or to the freeholders.

Legal battles have always been a feature of my projects, and they loomed large over George Arthur Road. It is often these bureaucratic tangles which have provided the main deterrents to residents lacking both legal knowledge and the cash to pay solicitors, so the community architect has to be able to tackle the law as part of the job.

In this case the Leasehold Reform Act looked as if it might offer some leverage. We understood that leases could be bought for ten times the cost of ground rent, but on closer inspection the Act was shown to be less than straightforward. There was a critical loophole, confirming what London, City and Westcliff had said, which allowed the freeholder to keep the property on expiry of the lease.

Denis Howell, a Labour MP in Birmingham, was called on for help in publicizing the case of leaseholders. He was sympathetic. Legal help was also enlisted, and the struggle began in earnest to persuade London, City and Westcliff to sell the freeholds either to one responsible landlord of the residents' choice or to each householder. They were persuaded, and disposed of some leases to those householders who wanted them, and the rest to the local COPEC Housing Trust.

At the same time we were fighting to obtain classification of the road as part of a Housing Action Area. After fifteen months of campaigning the council eventually conceded that we had a valid case and declared the HAA in February 1975.

Winning over the opposition

Work on modernization and general improvements began at the end of the year, and was eventually completed five years later. The local authority watched our progress closely and even adopted some of the ideas themselves – such as 'enveloping', which had first been used successfully at Black Road. This was a comprehensive approach which started renovation at one end of a terrace or street and worked its way house by house to the other end. It allowed all roofs, front garden walls and communal areas to be repaired in one go.

This process highlighted a fault in the 1969 Housing Act, which treated homes as individual entities. For example, it enabled a grant to be offered to reroof one mid-terrace house without taking adjoining properties into account. It had become clear that homes like these had to be tackled together to ensure a consistent standard of repair. Regrettably, the 1974 Act did nothing to discourage piecemeal renovation.

However, the council did get the message and paid us the compliment of adopting the George Arthur Road methods city-wide. Birmingham's Urban Renewal Department even declared that an envelope package should be used in all Housing Action Areas. Commercial property was also given a facelift in a joint effort by the council and the owners. Side by side with renovated homes in Saltley, restored shops and offices gave the whole area a new lease of life.

Having taken the initiative, the council, previously noted for its obdurate allegiance to a demolition and new building programme, was rapidly establishing a reputation for being an innovative force in saving properties. But this change of tack left many residents distrustful of the underlying motives. There was a poor response to offers of improvement grants and, despite the council's attempts to make more money available, it had still not managed to untangle the obstructive bureaucracy.

However, Birmingham led the country in demonstrating how the 1974 Housing Act could be used to the best advantage. And to its credit, it went to great lengths to encourage people to work together. A series of city-wide urban renewal offices were established, where local authority officers could easily be visited by residents' groups seeking advice. The scheme worked well, and people were noticeably more willing to speak to council representatives in small local offices than they had been to visit them at the town hall.

Facts behind the figures

Despite Birmingham's surprising success story, towns and cities in the rest of the country were showing few signs of solving the housing question. Inner city problems worsened during the mid-seventies and public faith in the state and architects plunged further. The government had a shrinking purse for building programmes, and while local authority spending had increased from £2.5 billion in 1974 to £3.5 billion in 1975, much of this was swallowed up in repaying government loans made for high-rise building.

Labour's Housing Minister, Reg Freeson, endorsed the 1974 Act and its encouragement of small-scale works. He stressed there was a need to move away from huge building projects; 'There must be an end to high-rise flats for families and the wholesale demolition of large tracts of our cities.' In the light of so many problems with tower blocks he questioned the value of huge, cheaply built schemes.

He also fully backed the repair and improvement of existing homes and agreed there was a need 'to reach a fuller understanding of local problems and find better ways of coping with them. We have enough research studies to demonstrate that wholesale bulldozing really does cost more money – to public authorities and to ordinary people alike – than the gradual redevelopment of existing cities.'

However, it fell to Anthony Crosland, Labour's Secretary of State for the Environment, to boost public confidence in state housing. In 1976 he announced that home building was still exceeding demolition each year, that between 1971 and 1974 some 220,000 new dwellings had been completed annually, and that there had been a net increase in households of some 180,000 between 1971 and 1976. These figures, coupled with the fact that national population figures had stabilized, were an indication, he said, that housing was more than keeping pace with requirements.

Reg Freeson added that new house-building figures would no longer be the sole barometer of housing progress. 'The days of massive crude housing shortages are gone,' he said.

The reality was quite different. Waiting lists for council housing were growing longer. There was increasing dissatisfaction with the slum clearance programme and strong criticism by residents of the poor-quality housing which replaced the Victorian terraces. Many local authorities were involved in major refurbishments of the new structures.

The housing action group Shelter added to the bleak picture with its damning report *Homes Fit for Heroes* – an ironic reference to Lloyd George's housing programme, set in motion after World War I. This investigation claimed there were half a million British homes unfit for human habitation. Even more damaging findings had appeared in another report entitled *The Inner Cities*. Published in 1975 by the London Council of Social Studies, and jointly funded by the Home Office, the Department of Employment and the Department of the Environment, the study focused attention on Brixton and the East End of London. Unemployment plus inadequate housing, particularly among the vulnerable black population, were identified as major causes for concern.

A state of collapse

The new types of building had dispensed with the traditional skills such as joinery, masonry and bricklaying, and sites were largely manned by unskilled labourers. The great rush to build ever faster was encouraged through bonus incentives. Quality was inevitably sacrificed and corners were cut in the effort to beat deadlines. Pride in craftsmanship was abandoned.

Failure of materials was another major problem, and a number of disasters in the early seventies showed that Ronan Point was no freak accident. In the autumn of 1973 Britain suffered its worst peacetime fire since the twenties when fifty people were burned to death at the Summerland Leisure Centre on the Isle of Man. Investigations showed that the magnitude of the disaster had been increased by the use of acrylic sheeting as external cladding. Poor design of escape routes also came in for serious criticism.

One of the most widely used building systems, known as CLASP, was another fire trap and led to the demise of countless schools. The system was constructed in a way that left spaces in between roofs and walls, which acted as natural flues and encouraged fire to spread at a frightening pace. In just one month in 1974 three schools were gutted in Derbyshire alone. Although measures were taken to make the structures safer, the following year Yarborough School in Lincoln burned to the ground in just twenty minutes.

Concrete, particularly the type known as high alumina cement

(HAC), and other kinds containing calcium chloride, was causing massive amounts of damage. The strength of HAC depended on both a precise water ratio in its mixing and being set at a specific temperature. Because it was so temperamental the material had been banned in France since 1943. But its use continued in the UK. By the mid-seventies some fifty to sixty thousand buildings were suspected of containing HAC concrete. Many, although they had been standing for a short time, were showing signs of stress and needed urgent and expensive repairs.

In 1973 the collapse of the entire assembly hall roof at London's Camden School for Girls was due to the failure of HAC; the concrete around the end of supporting beams had deteriorated. Just twenty-four hours earlier the hall had been filled with five hundred parents attending a meeting. The same type of concrete deterioration was detected at Manor School, Ruislip in the summer of 1975. Emergency repairs at a cost of £15,000 were undertaken; Hillingdon Council had already spent an additional £110,000 locating HAC in many of its other buildings.

A high calcium chloride content was found to be causing spalling in concrete – a flaking away of the surface – and to be rusting reinforcements at three blocks of council flats in Salford during the summer of 1975. They cost around £80,000 to repair. Urgent remedial work, due to spalling concrete, corroded steel and loss of structural strength, was identified at twenty-six crumbling Newcastle tower blocks that summer. The scale of the repair work needed was enormous, and was expected to cost several hundred thousand pounds.

The catalogue of disasters to hit the headlines in 1975 alone included decorative mosaic panelling falling from the IBM office block in Croydon; a new telephone exchange in Chester pulled down in mid-construction because of poor workmanship; employees evacuated from the Inland Revenue Office in New Malden, Surrey, when serious structural defects were found in the floors; the British Steel Corporation removing the top 30 metres from two cooling towers at Llanwern when wind caused the 110-metre-high structures to crack; and yet more cracks detected at new buildings including Centre Point and the Polytechnic of Central London.

Building protest

Complaints from the public about local authority tower blocks became more vociferous. They were the same congenital problems: leaking flat roofs, long windswept corridors, blind corners which made mugging easy, inefficient lifts, poor heating systems and inadequate sound insulation were universally loathed. Car parks were unsafe and too big. The acres of asphalt surrounding blocks made people afraid to leave their cars at the mercy of vandals. Open spaces were piled high with litter.

There were complaints, too, against zoning. Residents at the huge estates were alienated by it and disliked the fact that they had to travel long distances to shops, schools and even play areas. Newly designed town and city centres were hated because of the ugly, characterless office blocks and the dismal, windy, concrete shopping centres.

The press demanded that architects should be called to account for their ineptitude and inefficiency. Why were so many buildings so ugly? Why were they badly built? Why were tower blocks still going up when they were so strongly disliked? It had been proved long ago that the old streets housed just as many people in the same space as towers, so why were towers built in the first place? Why had so many cityscapes been unnecessarily scarred by office blocks which lay empty? Why had the public been ignored? Why did architects have so few answers?

It was clear that Modernism had solved nothing. After all, the public wasn't asking for great works of art. Most people weren't even asking for design of a particularly high standard. They wanted safe and pleasant surroundings – a home that was easy to maintain, a proper garden, the knowledge that their children could play safely nearby, and shops and schools within walking distance. And people love to be able to make their own mark – as has been demonstrated during the eighties when tenants have had the opportunity to buy their council houses. As you drive round any estate the home owners are easy to spot: they have added their own choice of doors and windows, pillars, porches and fancy garden walls. Some work, some don't but that's not the point – what matters is that individuals are expressing their own tastes and preferences in their own way. By the mid-seventies tenants had had enough of being told what was good for them.

For decades élitist designers had single-mindedly pursued Modernism. In the Corbusian tradition, most were convinced that their work was above criticism. When the new buildings first appeared they felt that public disapproval was unwarranted, but only to be expected: people were facing the shock of the new. The credo was that people would grow used to the towers and offices in the same way that they had grown accustomed to Victorian innovations.

Architects were on the defensive, saying they had been following the orders of councils and developers to build tall, build fast and build cheap. They also attacked local authorities for imposing unnecessarily restrictive planning demands and for failing to provide adequate maintenance for the buildings. But the volume of criticism was impossible to ignore and many architects, including myself, were forced to question our training and our role.

I had already changed direction from Modernist to community architect, even though it was evident that many of my colleagues were still stuck in the Modern Movement rut. So many of the ideas I had been taught at architecture school now appeared not simply naive, but actually harmful. I had been advised that it was best to work alone at the drawing desk: working closely with potential users could compromise original designs. Traditional buildings and materials had, according to Modernist doctrine, reached the end of their useful purpose; modern materials were the only way forward. Yet all this had been disproved during the community schemes.

Public criticism of Modernism was undoubtedly well founded. I felt angry at my narrow training. I blamed avaricious developers for promoting abuse of the new methods, but architects were to blame for so much bad design. However, not all designers worked in the same way, so it is important to draw distinctions between the different types. The seventies saw the design profession fragment into three distinct groups – sculptors, community architects and, by far the largest group, businessmen.

The sculptor architects

The sculptors were few, and worked exclusively on designing prestige projects. Their buildings, often in prime city centre sites, were quality-built with generous budgets. The sculptor was feted by his clients and vested with complete control.

Among the most dazzling sculptor architects who rose to fame in the seventies were Richard Rogers and Renzo Piano. Their most notable triumph was the building of the Pompidou Centre in Paris between 1972 and 1977. The ingenious idea of putting all mechanical services such as plumbing, ventilation and escalators on the outside captured imaginations. And the combined use of materials, such as brightly coloured plastics, metals and glass, has ensured the designers a place in the history books. Providing a startling contrast to the surrounding old Parisian buildings, it drew praise from many quarters while others simply loathed it. The Pompidou Centre rapidly became (and has remained) one of the most visited buildings in Europe.

Norman Foster was another of the rising stars. His Willis, Faber and Dumas offices in Ipswich, built between 1972 and 1975, were heaped with praise. A perfectionist and inspired designer, Foster used his wealth of engineering knowledge to produce a stunning and original building. He acknowledged the inspiration of Paxton's Crystal Palace in this building entirely clad in a curtain wall of toughened plate glass. During the day the glass serves to reflect the ancient market town buildings, but at night it takes on a life of its own as a glowing transparent box. The interior was extremely unusual for its time: it provides office space for 1300 people and yet has the feel of a luxury hotel. The central open-plan area on the ground floor is an atrium filled with plants, and from there escalators climb to the upper floors. Also included are facilities such as a gym, swimming pool, café bar, restaurant and landscaped roof garden.

Foster further enhanced his reputation with the 1974–8 Sainsbury Centre at the University of East Anglia in Norwich. The steel frame with beams and columns shaped like prisms, and the huge spans of glass, combine to give the structure a lightweight, almost ephemeral feel; the drama of its simplicity and the beautiful surroundings have guaranteed Foster success.

James Stirling, made famous in the sixties for his Cambridge University History Faculty, Florey Building and Leicester University Engineering Building, was rapidly gaining an international reputation. However, his early work involved considerable experimentation with new materials, which in turn introduced technical problems – leaking joints, and heating and air conditioning faults.

One of the most publicized disasters was his futuristic 1350-dwelling Southgate housing estate at Runcorn in Cheshire, built in 1975. It was soon nicknamed 'Legoland' by its occupants because of its extensive use of glass, reinforced plastic and 'Toytown'-style designs with porthole windows. These experimental and shoddy materials decayed rapidly and in early 1989 the condition of the estate was revealed to be so poor that it was threatened with demolition. The Runcorn Development Corporation, labouring under a burden of some £600,000 in annual repair bills, took the decision to demolish the buildings and clear the site. It had already spent over £3.5 million on maintenance during 1985–8.

In his defence, Stirling explained that the estate was designed at

Not built, India

IDEAL HOMES

Self-built, Lewisham

Rebuilt, Alexander Cottages, Spitalfields

Jerry-Built, South America

Designer-built, Søholm housing scheme, Denmark

Manchester School of Architecture

French housing at Marne-le-Vallée

a time when it was considered inappropriate to build new towns, such as Runcorn, in traditional styles. He added that his brief from the Development Corporation had been restrictive and un-compromising. It insisted on achieving a density of 100 per acre and to build, using pre-cast concrete, within a tight budget. The design had to include accommodation for 6500 people, one shop, one pub, and 1.5 car spaces per dwelling. 'It seems unfair that architects' input should today [1989] be considered as being primarily responsible for the lack of quality,' said Stirling. 'Ulti-mately it may well rest with the policy of successive governments building the maximum numbers for minimum cost, as quickly as possible.' At the time of writing, the residents have decided they don't want to be moved on again and are working with community architects to devise a £27 million rescue package for repairs to enable them to stay.

During the late seventies, however, Stirling's reputation was still intact and he had set aside purely industrialized materials in favour of more traditional ones. This new approach was demonstrated in the highly prestigious German commission for the new Staats-galerie in Stuttgart. The long, low building combined blocks of differing shapes, mingling elements of Classicism with some of the 'anything goes' styles of emerging Post-Modernism – Egyptian, Gothic, Roman, Greek, Arts and Crafts, vernacular, traditional, Art Nouveau – and was finished in small, coloured stone slabs. It is a building which has survived the test of time largely because it was well built on a hefty budget.

Another international architect, Jorn Utzon, was responsible for one of the world's most obviously 'sculptured' buildings – Sydney Opera House, completed in 1973. The work took sixteen years and building costs rose from an estimated $7 million to $70 million, but the finished structure, featuring huge white concrete tile-clad 'sails', won worldwide acclaim. However, as with the early Stirling buildings, pushing technology to the limits culminated in a massive repair bill – at just fifteen years old the Opera House now needs a $30 million facelift.

Community architects

My own chosen branch of the profession, community architecture, challenged what the majority of architects perceived as their role. They didn't work with the huge budgets and autonomy of the sculptors, nor were they interested in designing and rebuilding city centres. Instead they took the unorthodox, grass roots approach of working with people to save and renovate old housing and preserve communities.

Ralph Erskine had worked on one of the earliest projects in the UK at the Byker scheme in Newcastle during the late sixties and very early seventies. The project was enormous, covering 200 acres and housing ten thousand residents. Erskine set up an on-site office working from a disused funeral parlour. The tenants were invited to help devise designs and their children were involved in making models of the scheme. The biggest problem was to protect the estate from bitterly cold north winds and from the noise of a nearby major road.

The result was an enormous 'ribbon' block rising from between five and eight storeys, which became known as the Byker Wall, and a selection of low-rise buildings. The materials used included colourful red, yellow and brown bricks laid in patterns, and stained timber. Great attention was paid to the provision of playgrounds, landscaped public areas, shops, offices and social facilities. Familiar landmarks such as pubs and churches were left un-demolished during the land clearance and were incorporated within the scheme.

Building costs, even with the employment of full-time architects and involving time-consuming public consultation, worked out to be no greater than other, concrete-built municipal schemes providing homes for the same number of people. Such was its success and popularity with residents that, despite the fact that it was in the middle of a city, it won a Best Kept Village award shortly afterwards. My Black Road scheme in Macclesfield followed in 1972.

Also that year, in Scotland, a new style of architect advice shop – ASSIST – was opened. Founded in Govan, Glasgow by Jim Johnson, the grant-assisted scheme provided architects to help rehabilitate the depressed inner city area. These architects successfully managed to halt the mass demolition of old, run-down four-storey tenements and then helped tenants install new bathrooms and kitchens.

The seventies saw a rise in the numbers of people building their own homes, a trend which was largely helped by Walter Segal and his designs for easily constructed timber-framed houses. He had experimented with a number of different approaches and eventually built a prototype house in his own garden in Highgate, north London. His aim was to devise a house which could be built by someone with very little practical expertise, using only a basic range of tools. By 1978 his designs were perfected and fourteen families, including pensioners and single parents, on council waiting lists in Lewisham in south-east London made their own timber-framed homes. The popularity of self-building has continued to grow.

Business architects

Far outnumbering the other two arms of the profession, the business architect was greatly in demand. Here was the root of so much evil. Those who were prepared to toe the 'quick and cheap' line were highly successful at finding work. They offered slick packages irresistible to private developers and councils whose only concern was to see projects, designed to offer the maximum square footage, completed on time and within budget. Their clients were less concerned about aesthetics or taste than they were with their accounts departments.

I worked in Bernard Engle's London office at the start of the rise of the business architect, during the late sixties. The thinking that was evolving at that time set the tone for the following decade. It was clear that Engle, then working on plans for the Brent Cross shopping complex in north London, had no pretensions to create great sculptural objects. The aim was to satisfy developers and pick up the cheque in settlement for an efficient package.

One project I helped design was a shopping complex for Hammerson's, a firm of developers, at Southend-on-Sea. Here I had first-hand experience of how the system worked. The scheme was produced quickly on a tight budget, and constructed in concrete and steel. Hammerson's had devised a plan to keep costs to the absolute minimum by simply building a basic structure containing retail 'shells' which shop owners were to complete in their own finishes. The result was a hotch-potch of styles and qualities. It wasn't long before the building started to look unsightly. Cheap was clearly very nasty.

John Poulson epitomized all that was worst in the profession. His methods of acquiring contracts by bribery, and his subsequent come-uppance, have already been described. The results were some of the most soul-less, mass-produced buildings of the decade – the Airedale General Hospital near Keighley, the International Swimming Pool at Leeds, Helles and Vimy Barracks at Catterick, and the Dewsbury and Batley Technical Art College.

There were many other architects, including those working within the law and with a good reputation for design, who willingly complied with the quick-and-cheap philosophy. James Stirling's Runcorn estate, the failure of which has already been mentioned, was typical of its results. Some were quick, but not necessarily cheap, like the Commercial Union Building in the City of London, designed by Gollins, Melvin and Ward for the site formerly occupied by the Shell headquarters. To provide maximum floor space, the building was designed as a suspended structure around a central concrete core. Floors of lightweight steel were hung from cantilevered steel truss sections. The entire high-rise office tower was completed in just twenty-four weeks.

Another symbol of out-and-out commercialism was Owen

Luder's disastrous Tricorn Development, a vast, Brutalist concrete complex of shops, offices and flats which dominates the centre of Portsmouth. It was voted Britain's sixth worst building by *Observer* readers in June 1989. From the day it opened there were problems – many shops there have remained unleased. Luder defended his design by saying:

> The Tricorn has never been maintained and never filled up with shops. It was designed when the shopping market was buoyant, but the market slumped by the time it opened. History is littered with examples of where the avant-garde is booed and hissed by populists, only to find later that it's top of the pops. Architects should not be forced into the lowest common denominator. If you don't have an avant-garde, you don't have progress.

Unfortunately, what Luder and many other Modernists hadn't realized was that a good theory could be downright bad in practice. The argument put forward by many Modernists that innovation is essential and therefore, by implication, good, fails to recognize that innovation *can* be bad and that not all of it advances our civilization.

The empire strikes back

Not surprisingly the architectural profession found itself under fire, and, for the first time in its 140-year history, the Royal Institute of British Architects was called upon to take some action in self-defence. The Institute's council and members could hardly be unaware of the level of public dissatisfaction, and knew there was a clear need to improve their professional image.

Up until then the RIBA had been a rather stuffy, old-fashioned club which steered a safe course between politics and trouble. But now urgent measures had to be taken. In 1976 the president, Eric Lyons, spoke out in support of his fellow professionals, but also conceded that changes were necessary. 'I feel the profession has discharged its enormous responsibility to society very decently. The low status of the architect in Britain stems from a fashionable cult of philistinism. However, we must find better ways of solving building problems than those clumsy and inadequate measures of the past few years.'

A glimmer of hope lay in community architecture. People liked to keep their homes. The extraordinary thing is that local authorities took so long to recognize the potential for solving their problems cheaply, with little effort, and with the support of voters. And so in 1976, after the initial almost complete professional dismissal, the RIBA formed the Community Architecture Working Group (CAWG). It was composed of designers from both public and private sectors who were interested in exploring a new approach to building and regeneration.

As a committee member I helped outline the group's main objectives. We needed to find out the extent of existing help available to community groups and to identify how it could be improved. It soon became clear that demand far outweighed supply. The group felt that, because community projects represented good value for money in improving environments, more help should be offered, preferably funded by government, to enable self-help groups to derive maximum benefit from legislation to get projects underway. CAWG's aim was to act as a catalyst, providing advice and directing funds to schemes around the country.

Among the first of the group's practical contributions was the founding of an 'urban workshop' in Newcastle. In 1977 it teamed up with students at the city's school of architecture to run a city centre advice shop which provided information and support services, in architecture and planning, to community groups and individuals. Money from the RIBA and the government job creation programme paid for a staff of three architects whose services were augmented by students.

A tide of change was evident in architecture schools around the country. One poll, conducted by the *Architects' Journal* in the autumn of 1977, revealed that architectural students at around half of all British schools were involved in work on community projects. The schemes varied: for example, London's School of Environmental Studies designed and built a parents' building at Fleet School, Camden; the Hull School helped save sixty homes threatened with demolition in Beverley; the Architectural Association's diploma unit worked with a group of deaf people and built a meeting place in Swindon; and the Mackintosh School, Glasgow designed and built a playground for young hospital patients at Yorkhill.

Meanwhile, most urban areas showed little sign of the regeneration anticipated by the government, and the depth of the crisis was outlined in a White Paper entitled *The Policy for the Inner Cities*. Its findings reinforced everyone's worst fears: they highlighted poor environmental conditions, high unemployment, lack of opportunity and concentrated areas of social deprivation.

That same year my work took me to Belfast. It was like a war zone. Vandalism and neglect had taken their toll on properties. Architects worked in fortified offices, and builders were obliged to pay protection money. Councils had no hope of finding enough money for improvements, but the human potential was there. Many people were unemployed: they had time on their hands and could be given the incentive to rebuild for themselves.

Setting up shop

In 1978, shortly after becoming CAWG's chairman, I commissioned a report called *The Case for a National Community Aid Fund*; its aim was to explain the role that the profession could play. We concentrated on the restoration of run-down inner city areas. The bulldozer was outlawed. CAWG outlined the need for a

Community Aid scheme providing funds to pay architects working with community groups. It hoped to introduce a type of street corner architect shop based on the lines of Legal Aid offices and similar to those opened a few years earlier in Glasgow. I saw the individual architect acting rather like a lawyer or GP – offering advice and helping to raise the standard of people's health. I wanted the government to realize how strong an ally the architectural profession could be in improving the environment and general welfare of the population.

The report was presented to the RIBA's council meeting in April 1978, and it was with some trepidation that I went along to the meeting. However, my nerves were calmed by the enthusiastic introduction from Alan Meakle, Chief Architect for Hereford and Worcester County Council. He began:

> Growing economic and social pressures mean that for many architects the nature of their job will change. The day of the big battalions with their bulldozing power craze is going. Now it is the turn of the infantry.
>
> We must be moving towards an architecture for everyone, not just for those with the money to pay for it.
>
> Much is being done, but not enough. So a national fund is needed to help the poor acquire the skills of architects, just like the Legal Aid scheme and the National Health Service help them get across to the services of the other professions.

The report won unanimous support. It was then presented to the Labour government, which was asked to adopt its findings.

Failure of nerve

During 1978 Labour, under Callaghan's leadership, was flagging. The depression had bitten hard, unemployment was still rising,

104

and conditions in the inner cities had continued their dismal decline. There was growing recognition of urban problems, and of the fact that, far from being isolated, they affected whole areas. At the RIBA's 1978 conference in Liverpool discussions on housing topped the bill.

The GLC Housing Chairman, George Tremlett, launched a blistering attack on architects, accusing the profession of debasing London. 'Architecture has been devalued, standards have fallen and municipal architecture is now held in contempt by politicians.' He also blamed architects for forgetting that their work was an art form and that high-rise developments and their like were 'almost unspeakable in their ghastliness. As artists you should have said no, no, no. During the past fifteen years the GLC has built around 320 towers, trapping around 80,000 people. Especially tragic is the fact that people were happier where they were before.'

A private builder, Tom Baron, described the problems facing his profession. Since builders worked for profit, he said, they built what they could sell where it was wanted. Inner city sites were at the bottom of the priority list because they were expensive and because local authorities refused to release large enough sites to appeal to developers. He added candidly that spec builders had ruined much of the countryside with their standard brick boxes designed without architects. He argued that architects and builders should work together to produce inner city housing of a quality that the average house buyer looked for and found in suburbia.

Government plans were forwarded by the Housing Minister, Reg Freeson, who told us that a report advising local authorities on how to get good value for money in development projects was on its way. He was in favour of councils disposing of any land they could for private development, and he hoped to encourage more self-help on the part of tenants by making grants more easily available and by strengthening their security of tenure.

However, despite his optimism and encouragement the national picture looked dismal. Building work had virtually ground to a halt and the construction industry was reeling from some severe knocks. It had been used as an economic regulator – the Treasury was able to inflate or deflate the economy at a stroke by increasing or decreasing DoE building funds. After being encouraged to expand with such rapidity in the boom years of the sixties, building companies were now obliged to cope with a series of political and economic vacillations. Having forged partnerships with local authorities while working on high-rise projects, builders were forced to find work elsewhere when those council contracts dried up. There were town centre developments, but by the end of the decade even those were dwindling. Many companies were facing bankruptcy.

As the country prepared for a general election the administration made a last-ditch attempt to tackle the problems in Britain's cities. The Inner Urban Act was passed, which provided government support for new industrial development for the inner cities and an expansion of the state Urban Programme. And in a further effort to curry favour the government founded a construction lobby – the Group of Eight. It was designed to unite government with architects, surveyors, engineers, building materials producers, builders and unions in planning for the future. But continuing cutbacks in public spending on construction never gave it a chance of success.

The end of the seventies and a new party in power at Westminster saw the end of major municipal building projects; under Margaret Thatcher, the private sector was to receive all the available government encouragement, and so the Group of Eight was eventually disbanded ten years later. In May 1979 as the Conservatives took office there was a nationwide feeling of optimism, but very few suspected the turmoil which was to follow.

6 Cry For Help

The Tory election campaign had centred on cutting back public sector waste, stopping Britain spending beyond its means and putting an end to unwieldy bureaucracies. Unfortunately, it soon became clear that the Conservatives did not recognize the scale of inner city problems. No extra money was made available, and help for urban areas had to be sought in the private sector.

The depths of recession

By 1981, government attempts to grapple with urban decay through lightweight private investment had proved useless. The recession continued to bite hard. Unemployment, at its worst in the inner cities, had reached 2 million and was rising; council house maintenance was limited; and new public housing was simply not being built.

The *English Homes Condition Survey*, a government report produced by the DoE, identified some 4.3 million dwellings (almost a quarter of the housing stock in England) as being in a state of disrepair. Over a million were classified as unfit for human habitation. Just under a million had no basic amenities. One million required over £7000 to be spent on essential repairs, and the remainder needed repairs costing around £2500 to bring them up to a reasonable standard. An additional 670,000 homes, mostly in the inner cities, lay unoccupied.

However, even these shocking figures did not reveal the enormity of the problem. They failed to include one vital element – the new council estates, omitted because they were not considered old enough to need repairs. The total estimated cost of solving the problems ranged from £70 billion, in government figures, to £86 billion, according to the left-wing Association of Metropolitan Authorities.

There had also been a severe drop in the numbers of new homes being produced: in 1976 there had been almost 270,000 – of which 170,000 were council-built. In 1981 there were fewer than 150,000 – of which only a third were council-built. Local authority spending on housing was one of the early cuts introduced by the Conservatives. In the mid-seventies government money spent on housing had been approaching £8 billion a year, but by the early eighties it had fallen to little more than £3 billion, and in the eight years from 1973 the number of architects employed by local authorities had been slashed by 22 per cent from 6169 to 4826.

The private sector was not immune to the recession, and showed no signs of making up the shortfall in local authority housing by building more. Figures released showing construction spending as a percentage of overall gross domestic product put Britain, with 9.2 per cent (considerably less than in the previous decade), in seventh place in a league table behind Japan with 17.7 per cent, West Germany with 12.4 per cent, Canada with 11.4 per cent, Italy with 10.8 per cent, France with 9.8 per cent and the USA with 9.4 per cent.

The 1981 Census clearly showed that the poorest urban areas had been hardest hit by unemployment. Britain as a whole had lost around 2 million jobs between 1971 and 1981 – a rise from 2 per cent to 8 per cent. However, some inner city areas in Liverpool, Glasgow, Newcastle, Leeds, Sheffield, Belfast and Cardiff had unemployment rates running as high as 30 per cent.

Although spending on aid had increased – the Urban Aid Programme for example, had funds of £30 million in 1973–4 increased to £110–115 million in 1979 – it missed its target. It failed to unravel the tangle of bureaucracy and did not address the dual problems of solving unemployment and improving housing. A great deal of this money was frittered away on administration.

Brixton – on the front line

The despair bred from poor housing, unemployment and lack of opportunity was to prove a volatile mixture. On 12 April 1981 a riot started in Brixton which lasted for two days. Ugly scenes were repeated in Southall in west London, Toxteth in Liverpool, Handsworth in Birmingham, St Paul's in Bristol and Moss Side in Manchester. At first the problem was blamed on a few trouble-makers. But the scale of the disorders and their coverage by television soon dispelled that illusion. Brixton, so close to the very centre of our capital city, shocked government and people. Lord Scarman, a former High Court Judge and first chairman of the Law Commission, was appointed to conduct a public inquiry specific-ally into the Brixton disorders.

The findings were published seven months later. Lord Scarman dismissed the convenient excuse that a small criminal element had been responsible, and attacked instead the environment that had spawned it:

> . . . the dreams of modern architects and planners do not necessarily provide any more of a setting for social harmony than do the run-down Victorian terraces. . .on the contrary they give rise to problems which terrace houses avoid.

The Scarman Report was one of the first official documents to admit the failure of modern architecture.

Brixton's problems were acute. The local authority, the London Borough of Lambeth, had its already limited resources stretched to breaking point. Of all households in the borough 20 per cent were owner-occupied, 33 per cent were privately rented and 45 per cent were owned by either Lambeth, the GLC or housing associations. There were almost twenty thousand families on the council waiting list; at least 10 per cent of all households were overcrowded, with two or more families living in one unit; twelve thousand dwellings had been classified as unfit; and a further eight thousand lacked basic amenities such as inside toilets.

For Lord Scarman, the surprise was not that there had been a riot in Brixton, but that it hadn't happened earlier. The warnings about inner city decay made at the 1978 RIBA conference were now seen in a fresh light. In assessing the other riot areas it took no extraordinary powers of observation to notice that they were all poor and suffering from high employment. While the sparking point had been different in each case, deprivation was clearly a common factor. In his summing-up Lord Scarman quoted from President Johnson's address to the nation following the series of American riots in 1968:

> The only genuine long-range solution for what has happened lies in an attack mounted at every level upon the conditions that breed despair and violence.

Tarzan in the urban jungle

The government was advised in the Scarman Report to restructure itself – to take sections from a number of ministries and form them into a single department with the aim of making a concerted attack on poverty and deprivation. The plan was to introduce a 'bottom-up' approach starting with the improvement of homes, giving people dignity and teaching them skills through carrying out their own repairs. This was intended to replace the government's 'top-down' policy, which had imposed a rigid structure of plans, rules and projects to encourage the creation of jobs in the hope that the poor, once employed, would be better equipped to look after themselves.

However, the government was unwilling to take that sort of drastic action. It preferred to fantasize that it was confronted with a short-term problem. But Lord Scarman's findings must have come as a considerable shock. Why else was the report effectively buried – left unheeded by the very body which had commissioned it? Meanwhile Environment Minister Michael Heseltine had come under fire for the state of inner city decay, and he set about preparing his own report on problems in Liverpool.

The Toxteth riots raged for three days from 3 July. Just over two weeks later Heseltine, accompanied by Tim Sainsbury from his own department and Timothy Raison from the Home Office, went on an unprecedented two-week fact-finding visit. The cavalcade of shining ministerial cars, hotly pursued by an entourage of photographers, reporters and television crews, was a bizarre sight among the derelict and heavily vandalized estates of Croxteth and Toxteth. Not surprisingly, many Liverpudlians treated the tour with nothing but scorn. The Labour-controlled Merseyside County Council denounced the trip as a massive public relations stunt. It was hardly a subtle undercover operation and was soon dubbed by the locals the Heseltine Roadshow. But despite the jokes Heseltine did put considerable effort into trying to understand the situation. He went on walkabouts and insisted on meeting with local groups and officials. Most people were naturally anxious to know how much money the government would promise the city, but Heseltine dodged these questions by saying he could offer no crock of gold. Mrs Thatcher had made it brutally clear that large amounts of money had already been pumped into Merseyside, and that public spending constraints applied equally to all parts of Britain. The Conservatives were loath to make riot zones special cases for fear that other poor urban areas would orchestrate more trouble to attract government money. I was appalled at this display of cynical logic.

However, by the end of his stay Heseltine had won the grudging respect of some of his most hardened critics in the city. Liverpool had never before seen a government minister so determined to talk with and listen to people, and everyone wondered what would happen when he reported to the Cabinet.

The best-laid plans

Heseltine returned to London with his grand plan to tackle inner city problems by restructuring ministry departments, to co-ordinate cross-ministry spending and to encourage joint public and private sector projects. The main thrust of his ideas was to use public investment as a trigger to encourage private spending. These were useful initiatives, but, as both he and Lord Scarman quickly discovered, proposals brought back by missionaries were not well received by those who hadn't seen the natives at first hand.

Every single one of Heseltine's ideas was chucked out at the mid-October Cabinet meeting. But shortly afterwards a task force was set up, and Heseltine was charged with implementing drastically watered-down plans during a twelve-month spell in his newly created role as Minister for Merseyside. Extra spending was ruled out, but some additional help was offered in the shape of a band of civil servants from the Manpower Services Commission and the departments of the Environment, Transport and Industry.

The new minister voiced his dismay at the complete lack of understanding. Once again the rules were being dictated by Whitehall without taking local needs into account. He was quoted as saying:

It is astonishing that this initiative, which is supposed to establish closer links between Merseyside and local authorities, was not discussed in advance with council leaders or officials.

He also managed to cause a stir among ministers and other colleagues when he proclaimed that 'it took a riot to make plain the gravity of inner city problems'. However, he tried to make the best of a bad situation and managed to extract promises of assistance from around twenty private industries, who agreed to second senior members of staff to work with government to encourage co-operation between the public and private sectors.

Heseltine had his work cut out. By the time he was appointed Minister for Merseyside in 1982 Liverpool was a dying city; the days of its former glory as a prosperous and thriving major port were gone. In twenty years around a third of the population had disappeared, leaving just half a million inhabitants. Factory closures were commonplace and almost sixty thousand people were registered unemployed – 40 per cent of them had been jobless for over a year, and 13 per cent hadn't worked for more than three years. In 1978 the *Liverpool Post* had reported that employment exchanges had virtually given up trying to find jobs for the hardcore unemployed.

Opportunity knocked

Heseltine's initiatives included several training schemes for local unemployed youngsters, an information technology centre to encourage the use of computers, plans for some new housing, the establishment of an annexe to the Tate Gallery, and an international garden festival to be held at a site just south of Toxteth. Unfortunately they did no more than scratch the surface of the problem.

Despite the fact that most of the schemes lacked real substance the minister had successfully managed to woo large sections of the community, including many who had never voted Tory in their lives. People admired his individual stand. He said:

I look to the top when I look for failure, to those who have the power and the responsibility. . . . By and large if society is to advance by evolution it depends on those with power. If it is to advance in any other way it will change by revolution.

The best-remembered of his projects was undoubtedly the

Garden Festival. But, although it attracted media attention and visitors to the city, it achieved nothing more substantive. The grandiose multi-million-pound scheme was devised to promote the use of derelict land and to inspire urban regeneration. To visitors it had all the appearance of success. Heseltine hoped the project would encourage the involvement of local people, particularly the unemployed, but his directives were ignored and contracts went almost exclusively to outsiders. Builders were given no encouragement to train the local unemployed. They wanted to complete the job quickly and so they brought in their own staff. Even the catering facilities were awarded to outsiders: not one hot dog stand or whelk stall was run by Liverpudlians. The only area where local initiative thrived was in the black market. Countless people managed to build new walls, paint their houses and resurface their drives with the spoils from the Festival site. I was told that the easiest method of finding my way to the exhibition was to follow the route of the newly asphalted driveways.

The mismanagement and throwing away of opportunities were both incomprehensible and unforgivable. The articulate and competent population, which should of course have been the driving force of the regeneration process, was taunted by watching the excesses of the massive scheme and had to be content with taking the scraps.

In theory the Tate of the North was another good idea. The redirection of art centres from rich to poorer areas, as an instrument of revival, had worked successfully in America. But here again, in Liverpool the potential of the local workforce was ignored. Heseltine's ideas were scuppered by Whitehall.

Nevertheless the Royal Albert Dock conversion scheme was an excellent reuse of an old building. It showed that a Victorian warehouse could be imaginatively adapted for different use and it brought new life to an otherwise dead waterfront immediately south of the Royal Liver Building. Most importantly for Liverpudlians, it was an act of faith: Liverpool had been established as a port; with the collapse of the city's economy it was the port that became the first area of dereliction. The place then festered from the shoreline inwards. Lack of jobs meant lack of wages; lack of wages meant that a large number of people relied on the state for hand-outs. Just as deprivation had set in from the shoreline, perhaps the renovation of the Albert Dock would reverse this trend and renovation and upgrading would spread eastwards from the docks.

All the president's men

In the summer of 1981 Owen Luder was elected president of the RIBA. It was an election that shook the old guard. For the entire 147-year history of the institute presidents had been chosen according to a system that seemed more appropriate to a gentleman's club – by virtue of the fact that it was their 'turn'. However, East End-born Luder issued a daring challenge to the council's candidate, Andrew Derbyshire, and attracted sufficient support to be voted president. He was outspoken on inner city strife and did not fudge the suggestion that a new approach to regeneration was crucial. 'Something has got to happen – the talking has got to stop,' he declared. It was time to relax restrictive planning controls. Tax incentives should be introduced to entice private investors into inner cities.

Luder put promotion of the profession at the top of his list of priorities and set aside £10,000 for this purpose. I was appointed his vice president for public affairs, in which capacity I had to scrutinize the role of architects and establish how the profession was perceived by the public – sadly this did not need extensive research on my part.

The small band of community architects had welcomed the proposals of Lord Scarman and Michael Heseltine, but the main body of architects, represented by officials at the RIBA, remained in a quandary. Some decided to ignore the situation completely, but a growing number began to acknowledge the faults of Modernism and its profound contribution to urban disarray.

There was general agreement among the the most enlightened that government cut-backs had been harmful and that Whitehall had failed to take adequate control of the situation. There was also serious concern for the ailing building industry. For two decades it had been told what to build, where to build and how to build. Its income had been heavily subsidized. Suddenly, all that had changed. Construction companies had either gone bankrupt or were looking for contracts abroad. It was infuriating to see that, at a time when the inner cities needed most help, the builders were being squeezed out.

Better than CS gas

I traced the three-year-old report from CAWG and pulled it down from the shelves; its proposals were resuscitated to set up a fund for making professional services available to small groups. In the August 1981 issue of the *RIBA Journal* appeared a feature head-lined: 'Better than CS gas': it announced that the Institute would provide £10,000 to fund a pilot urban renewal project. Our target scheme was to create a community centre near Bolton at Highfield Hall. People in the area wanted their own small local centre – they didn't want to travel to the centre of Bolton either for meetings or to play a game of table tennis.

By November 1981 Teresa Borsuk, a graduate of London's Bartlett School of Architecture, had been appointed to head the project. Like all community architects she would be on call twenty-four hours a day and would be the main co-ordinator working with the community group, the local council, contractors, builders, the Manpower Services Commission, the press, the elderly farmer who had lived on the land, and the teenagers – once accused of vandalism – who were queuing up to help.

When Teresa arrived the site comprised a series of derelict buildings – an eighteenth-century farmhouse, a Victorian barn and surrounding paddocks. The community was enthusiastic, and soon additional funding was secured from the Manpower Services Commission and through an Urban Aid grant. Progress was slow through a bitter winter, but Teresa persevered. And, by convincing the group that the project's success lay exclusively in their hands, she managed to sustain their motivation. Work was swiftly completed the following summer (the tenth anniversary of community architecture in Britain), and the hall was opened by Tom King, Minister for Local Government and Environmental Services.

Small change

King showed a genuine concern for the welfare of small communities and was keen to encourage self-help schemes. In 1982 he set up the Urban Initiatives Fund (UIF) to help pay for technical and professional advisers to community groups; this idea sprang from discussions during the European Campaign for Urban Renaissance. His action demonstrated a significant government shift in promoting the voluntary sector. He admitted that:

> public money will never do all the jobs because there is such a massive amount to be done. The government will do what it can, but its skill is to get the maximum gearing with other funds coming in to support projects. Under the squeeze, local authorities tended to cut the voluntary side to protect their own projects.

He added that his policy, in line with government thinking, was to cut out waste and help in a cost-effective way to encourage projects that were self-financing.

The UIF worked on the basis of making grants available which had to be matched, pound for pound, by applicants. However, its major failing was that only £100,000 of government money was allocated per annum. (By comparison, the Community Technical Services Agency in Liverpool alone required some £61,000 a year.)

Heaven – and Hell – in Hackney

Despite the financing problems a variety of different approaches to renovation were gaining recognition. Forward-thinking councils decided to adopt community-led schemes. In Hackney in east London two identical blocks of flats, Lea View House and Wigan House, were restored in different ways – one used the traditional council method and the other followed the community route.

Both blocks had been built in 1939 and were then described as 'Heaven in Hackney'. Architectural writer Nikolaus Pevsner was a little more restrained in his praise: 'Uncommonly well designed,' he said. Each block was five storeys high and consisted of 300 units. The flats had modern kitchens, hot and cold running water and a lavatory. Communal facilities were lavish and included a community hall, a bowling green, tennis courts, a laundry, several porters and a resident caretaker.

However, in time running costs were cut, the bowling green was tarmaced over, the porters and caretaker lost their jobs and the blocks fell into a state of decay. By the end of the seventies it was classed as a sink estate. The tenants grew angry at the rotten conditions, the vandalism, the muggings and the filth, and formed a residents' association. They approached Hackney Council and demanded to be included on the priority list for improvements. The main drive behind the move was to escape, because the residents knew they would have to be rehoused during the improvement works.

That was not to happen. At the end of 1980 architects Hunt Thompson were appointed to restore Lea View House. Residents prepared to move out, but a fresh round of government cut-backs resulted in a radical change of plan. The council had no money to move people and announced that they would have to stay during the renovation period. The tenants were furious, and demanded complete control over what was going to happen to their homes.

This was the start of the first community refurbishment of a council block. Some of the bad feeling against architects was dispersed when the site office opened and residents were invited to take part in meetings discussing the works. Their trust grew as they realized their opinions were being listened to.

By 1981 proposals were ready. The Lea View building, set around a courtyard, was to be completely restructured internally, making ground-level 'houses' with gardens and front doors facing on to surrounding streets. Internal staircases were to be wall-papered and carpeted, elderly tenants would be housed in sheltered accommodation, some flats were to be designed specifically for the disabled, and everyone could choose how their place would be decorated. Externally the courtyard was to be landscaped, lift towers would be built with decorative brickwork, there would be pitched roofs, and all windows were to be replaced.

Work progressed with continual tenant involvement through 1981 and was eventually complete in the spring of 1982. The success of this particular project was all the more remarkable when comparisons were made with the council's own improvement carried out at the same time and at the same cost on the neighbouring Wigan House.

Some 90 per cent of the Lea View residents said that before refurbishment they had wanted to move out. Afterwards every single person said they were very happy with the estate, their own block and their own flat or house.

Around 70 per cent of tenants said their health had improved since completion, and 95 per cent said their nerves were better;

70 per cent were smoking less. There were no complaints about damp, and only 8 per cent were still afraid of using the lifts. Vandalism, mugging and burglary had been virtually eliminated, fuel bills were halved and communal areas stayed clean and litter-free.

The picture was very different at Wigan House. Just 30 per cent of tenants said they were happy with their new-look homes. Some 70 per cent said their health had worsened; 60 per cent felt their nerves were worse; 65 per cent were smoking more heavily; 65 per cent complained of damp problems; and 48 per cent were afraid of using the lifts. Within just six months of the refurbishment the block had reverted to its former slum condition.

The Eldonians

Around this time self-help schemes were also making their debut. One of the most heavily publicized was run by a group of Liverpool residents who came to be known as the Eldonians, after one of the local streets. Their project was the largest and most comprehensive ever run by council tenants.

Living by the Vauxhall entrance to the Mersey Tunnel, these people had for a long time suffered unemployment and poor living conditions. But the situation took a nose dive in 1980 when the area's largest employer, Tate and Lyle, closed its sugar refinery with a loss of 1700 jobs. The following year saw the area hit badly again because of the precarious state of local politics and rioting.

Fed up with being political pawns, the residents decided to take their housing problems into their own hands. They formed the Eldonian Housing Co-operative, then the largest in Britain, and set out to build 145 homes to rehouse families living in decaying inter-war tenement blocks. They managed to persuade Tate and Lyle to hand over its disused 22-acre factory site and began to draw up plans for the £4.5 million Eldonian Village. The project included the building of fair-rent and shared-ownership homes, canal-based industries and community facilities.

However, the closure of yet another factory and several small businesses left residents unable to afford ownership, and the scheme was revised to provide fair-rent houses, bungalows and flats together with shops and a community centre. The all-women design committee worked for over eight months on plans for the different types of homes they wanted.

Major obstacles were soon put in the way of progress when the Militant Labour Party gained control of the council in May 1983. The politicians saw self-help schemes as a threat to council housing, and attempts were made to curtail the Eldonians' plans. Eventually, after lengthy negotiation, the council was given some of the newly built houses and the work continued.

Despite all the setbacks, over a hundred had been completed in some four years. The Eldonians had shown that, with a huge amount of faith and liberal helpings of patience, much could be gained in the face of adversity. They also proved that, although self-help was a slow process, residents finished up gaining a tremendous sense of achievement, and made-to-measure, quality-built homes in an area they knew and liked.

Monstrous carbuncles

The Falklands conflict in 1982 provided a dramatic distraction from domestic problems. It occurred to me then that, just as the post-war housing programme had been run like a military operation, the Conservatives could have recycled the Falklands War Cabinet to tackle the cities.

However, by the time of the 1983 election urban areas did feature again in the Conservative manifesto. Michael Heseltine announced that the total resources devoted to the inner city programme, taking into account the extra fund for the Urban

Development Corporations of Merseyside and London Docklands, were higher than ever before – rising from £206 million in
1980 to £334 million for 1982–3.

By the summer of 1984 the national economy had shown an
upturn. Although council building was at a virtual standstill, the
private sector, emerging from the doldrums of the recession, was
beavering away. There was a rash of new construction sites
around the country.

Councils had abandoned the construction of towers: the small
amount of public housing being built consisted mostly of low-rise
structures. Meanwhile the private sector was concentrating on
easily marketable, traditional-style brick homes. Experimental
design was saved for the more prestigious projects, where Post-
Modernism and high-tech ruled.

Terry Farrell's humorous and colourful Post-Modern TV-am
building in Camden spawned countless imitations – not least in
shopping centres. And echoes of the Rogers/Piano high-tech
Pompidou Centre could be found in projects such as the award-
winning Elswick Pool and Park, Newcastle, and the Ulster Folk and
Transport Museum. The latest Rogers scheme – the Lloyd's
Building in the City of London – was also well under way.

Restoration of old buildings was particularly big business. For
example, the successful conversion of disused old market buildings in Covent Garden to a thriving shopping centre was recognized by the Otis Award for Urban Design; similarly, a refurbishment of the market hall and cobbled streets at the heart of
Chesterfield in Derbyshire scooped a Royal Institute of Chartered
Surveyors/*Times* conservation award. Dilapidated dockside
warehousing in London, Liverpool, Bristol and Chatham was
also being restored and had become extremely fashionable for
housing and shopping/leisure complexes.

The architectural profession had changed significantly. In
response to the criticisms of the previous decade it was no longer
populated entirely by elitists. And, through initiatives such as the
community projects, the advent of the more widely appealing

styles of Post-Modernism and high-tech, plus the popular refurbishment schemes, architects had regained some measure of public respect.

But despite its new-found boost of confidence, the profession was to receive a blow from an unexpected quarter. On 30 May the RIBA held a gala evening at Hampton Court Palace to celebrate its 150th anniversary, to which all the leading lights of the architectural world were invited. The guest of honour and principal speaker was the Prince of Wales. The effects of what he said then have been deeply felt, and have undoubtedly been instrumental in initiating one of the most significant changes in the history of modern architecture by opening up public debate on designs for major new buildings. The Prince also used the occasion to give community architecture the royal seal of approval.

I was then still RIBA vice-president of public affairs and, because of the gala, was staying in London with the current president, Michael Manser. On the day Michael was noticeably anxious about something, but it wasn't until late in the afternoon that I realized his nerves were connected with the contents of the Prince's speech. Copies had been circulated to the press and embargoed for publication until the following morning. The first anyone at the RIBA knew of its details was when a reporter from *The Times* called the secretary, Patrick Harrison, asking for his reaction to the Prince of Wales's attack on architects. There was a flurry of activity, followed by panic.

Both Michael and Patrick were clearly amazed that the Prince, who had after all been invited to celebrate 150 glorious years of achievement, was going to stand up and criticize his hosts. A stream of telephone calls was made to the Palace in an attempt to persuade the Prince to modify his speech. No assurances of a change were forthcoming.

When the assembled company finally shuffled into the Fountain Court, there were a few anxious faces. As the Prince drew his notes from his pocket he smiled, and it was obvious from the expression on Michael's face that he feared the worst. Our guest of honour began by talking about Prince Albert's fascination with architecture, his love of embellishment, his personal involvement with the great buildings of Osborne and Balmoral and his designs for farm buildings and interiors. He went on to describe the changing attitudes to buildings from the past:

> For at last people are beginning to see that it is possible, and important in human terms, to respect old buildings, street plans and traditional scales, and at the same time not to feel guilty about a preference for façades, ornaments and soft materials. At last, after witnessing the wholesale destruction of Georgian and Victorian housing in most of our cities, people have begun to realize that it *is* possible to restore old buildings, and, what is more, that there are architects willing to undertake such projects.

Then came his searing attack on the profession and the Modernist approach, followed by words of praise for community architecture:

> For far too long, it seems to me, some planners and architects have consistently ignored the feelings and wishes of the mass of ordinary people in this country. Perhaps. . .it is hardly surprising as architects tend to have been trained to design buildings from scratch – to tear down and rebuild. Except in interior design courses, students are not taught to rehabilitate, nor do they ever meet the ultimate users of buildings in their training – indeed, they can often go through their whole career without doing so. Consequently a large number of us have developed a feeling that architects tend to design houses for the approval of fellow architects and critics, not for the tenant. . . .
>
> To be concerned about the way people live, about the environment they inhabit and the kind of community that is created by that environment should surely be one of the prime

requirements of a really good architect. It has been most encouraging to see the development of community architecture as a natural reaction to the policy of decamping people to new towns and overspill estates where the extended family patterns of support were destroyed and the community life was lost. Now, moreover, we are seeing the gradual expansion of housing co-operatives, where the tenants are able to work with an architect of their own who listens to their comments and their ideas and tries to design the kind of environment they want, rather than the kind which tends to be imposed upon them without any degree of choice.

This sort of development, spear-headed as it is by such individuals as a vice president of the RIBA Rod Hackney and Ted Cullinan – a man after my own heart, as he believes strongly that the architect must produce something that is visually beautiful as well as socially useful – offers something very promising in terms of inner city renewal and urban housing, not to mention community garden design. Enabling the client community to be involved in the detailed process of design rather than exclusively the local authority, is, I am sure, the kind of development we should be examining more closely. Apart from anything else, there is an assumption that if people have played a part in creating something, they might conceivably treat it as their own possession and look after it, thus making an attempt at reducing the problem of vandalism. What I believe is important about community architecture is that it has shown 'ordinary' people that their views are worth having; that architects and planners do not necessarily have the monopoly of knowing best about taste, style and planning. . . . I can't help thinking how much more worthwhile it would be if a community approach could have been used in the Mansion House Square project. It would be a tragedy if the character and skyline of our capital city were to be further ruined and St Paul's dwarfed by yet another giant glass stump. . . .

What . . . are we doing to our capital city now? What have we done to it since the bombing during the war? What are we shortly going to do to one of its most famous areas – Trafalgar Square? Instead of designing an extension to the elegant façade of the National Gallery which complements it and continues the concept of columns and domes, it looks as if we may be presented with a vast municipal fire station. . . . I would understand better this type of High-Tech approach if you demolished the whole of Trafalgar Square and started again with a single architect responsible for the entire layout, but what is proposed is like a monstrous carbuncle on the face of a much-loved and elegant friend. . . . Why can't we have those curves and arches that express feeling in design? What is wrong with them?. . .

In this 150th anniversary year, which provides an opportunity for a fresh look at the path ahead. . .may I express the earnest hope that the next 150 years will see a new harmony between imagination and taste and in the relationship between the architects and the people of this country.

The immediate reaction, after muted applause, was a mixture of surprise and some outrage. Dinner followed and much of the conversation for the rest of the evening was centred on the Prince's attack.

After dinner I was told that the Prince wanted to see me in one of the ante-rooms to discuss his speech. This was our first meeting. The Prince said he was totally committed to the idea of helping people capitalize on their energy and resources to help combat social problems. I was heartened by his enthusiasm, particularly for community architecture – he had not visited a project, but was clearly well briefed. His desire to play a more active role himself led me to invite him to visit Black Road in Macclesfield, and he accepted.

The following day the media were full of stories about Prince Charles's outburst. Michael Manser was quoted as saying he was 'a bit surprised', and many architects criticized the Prince for attacking the two major new proposals, which were subject to public inquiry, in front of Environment Secretary Patrick Jenkin who was among the guests. There was concern that the Prince's pronouncements would prejudice planning decisions for both the National Gallery extension and Mansion House Square. The press soon latched on to the 'monstrous carbuncle' description, which has since become a catchphrase for ugly buildings.

Down to business

Prince Charles came to Macclesfield in February 1985. His visit was a red-letter day for the Black Road residents. The Prince was relaxed and spent a long time talking to people, walking round their homes and finding out exactly how the work had been tackled.

Two weeks later he recounted his experiences and expressed his hopes for regenerating inner cities in his second major speech on architecture. This was delivered in his capacity as a guest of the Institute of Directors to an audience of industrialists at the Albert Hall in London. The Prince stressed the need for more help from industry in revitalizing urban areas:

> The long-term decline of the British manufacturing industry has accelerated drastically in the last couple of decades and has left a trail of devastation. The desperate plight of the inner city areas is well known, with the cycle of economic decline leading to physical deterioration and countless social problems. It is only when you visit these areas that you begin to wonder how it is possible that people are able to live in such inhuman conditions.

He praised the success of community projects and then called for more support from industry:

Private, public and nationalized businesses should have a vested interest in building up socially and financially stable communities who will eventually become customers. Otherwise the potential long-term problems of social unrest will be to their detriment, should such conditions be exacerbated. The industry of this country will also suffer the kind of damage we can ill afford. Above all else we must ensure that the public and private sectors are interdependent.

Directors of private businesses have a vital role to play in securing the future of inner city areas. For instance, many own land and buildings that are going to waste and which could be made available to trusts to provide housing and some workspace for small firms. Retired managers could also make valuable contributions to trusts by providing managerial skills.

If we continue to ignore old antagonisms we shall very quickly end up as a fourth-rate nation with a standard of living even lower than the rest of Europe.

From Brixton to Broadwater Farm

Immediately after Prince Charles's speech the government announced a new City Action initiative linking the Department of the Environment, the Manpower Services Commission and the Department of Trade and Industry. I was invited by the Prince to organize a series of dinners at Kensington Palace, where during the following two years architects, business people and academics in architecture and planning gathered to exchange views and ideas for urban revival.

These dinners were held in the light of continuing government cut-backs. Rate capping had been introduced in the mid-eighties as a means of curbing local authority spending. Central government set each authority a limit on the maximum rate in the pound

SHOP HORROR

Above: 'Fortress' Fine Fayre, Newcastle

Below: Oxford Street 'Disneyland' Plaza

THE BANDWAGON ROLLS...

Prince Charles and Rod Hackney: sharing a vision

that it could levy. The authorities hardest hit were those in the poorest areas, usually Labour-controlled. Now government decided to increase rate capping, and much of the work that councils needed to carry out on their housing had to be further scaled down. At the same time the government's Housing Investment Programme budget was reduced and council building was hit again.

Such was the desperate shortage of cash that some authorities, including Liverpool City Council, devised ingenious ways to supplement their incomes by seeking funds from abroad. There had been an increase in inner city funding, but much of this was invested in the two development corporations in London and Liverpool. And yet, despite all government inducements, the private sector still showed few signs of helping to regenerate the poorest areas.

In the summer and autumn of 1985 there were violent outbursts in the Handsworth area of Birmingham and the St Paul's district in Bristol. But the worst displays of frustration and desperation took place in October in north London, at Broadwater Farm, Tottenham. A woman called Cynthia Jarrett died during a police raid on her flat, and in the two days of running battles that followed the estate was destroyed, many people were injured and one policeman, PC Colin Blakelock, was murdered. Agonized inquiries were initiated to establish the causes of such vicious and destructive behaviour. Social and racial problems were examined along with the design, construction and history of the estate. Once again, architects were drawn into the political arena.

The flames of Broadwater Farm highlighted so much that was wrong with council estates. Plans for the development had first been suggested in the mid-sixties. Even then there was local objection, because the chosen site was a popular allotment area. Opposition was so strong that residents employed a lawyer to present their case. He complained about the unsuitability of the site, which was built over a river that had a tendency to flood after heavy rain. The designers countered his protests, saying they would raise the blocks on stilts – so already the ground level was reduced to a 'dead', dark, wasteland area set aside for car parking and building supports.

The Labour government of 1965 had been locked into the post-war programme and instructed the London Borough of Haringey's architects to produce a thousand housing units per year. Scandinavian industrialized building systems were very much in vogue, and the factory-produced Larsen-Neilsen method, the one used at Ronan Point, was recommended. Indeed Ronan Point's builders – Taylor Woodrow-Anglian – also won the contract.

One consequence of government pressure was that the design and building of the estate was largely taken out of the hands of the council's own architects. The attractions to the local authority were the familiar ones – speed and cheapness. Contractors could simply be handed the work; it was then their responsibility to find a labour force and complete within budget and on time.

Building was started in June 1967. It was interrupted briefly after the collapse of Ronan Point, but work resumed after the dust had settled. The estate even won a DoE award for good housing in 1971, and the twelfth and final block was eventually completed in 1973. The 21-acre estate comprised ten low-rise blocks of between four and six storeys high, with two eighteen-storey towers and a small group of two-storey houses, providing a total of almost 1100 units housing over 3000 people. The original design had included shops, a pub, a launderette and surgeries for a doctor and dentist, but these never materialized because the money ran out. They were considered expendable luxuries. From the very first day, then, services were inadequate for the numbers of people involved.

Roy Limb, proud chairman of Haringey's planning committee at the time, was quoted as saying: 'Broadwater Farm will be an everlasting memorial to my committee.' He could not have predicted the irony of his remark.

Despite the lack of promised public amenities, many of the early residents were initially content: the flats were warm and quiet, with good views across London. But the picture soon changed. The estate, like so many others, quickly became run down and neglected. Structural defects started to show. Water seeped through the roofs and walls, cockroach infestation proved difficult to contain and disrepair prompted a stream of complaints.

In 1981 residents drew up a petition asking the council to spend more on improvements – burglary was common and security poor, lifts were frequently broken, vandalism was rife, window frames had rotted, doors hung off their hinges and the place was filthy. It was the same old story.

One resident, Joanne George, who later became chairperson of the tenants' association, told the riot inquiry about the condition of the home she was offered at the time;

> The flat I was allocated was in a really bad state of repair, there was no kitchen sink, no kitchen cupboard and a hole in the floor, it was just horrendous. It looked to me like squatters had lived there. All the passages had graffiti and stains, it was absolutely disgusting, and I was told there was no money for decorating.
>
> The local press made Broadwater Farm their target for shock reports. Every single problem in Haringey, or even the whole of Tottenham, seemed to emanate from the estate.

Broadwater Farm was the subject of a DoE report into 'difficult-to-let' estates. Its popularity was described as having taken 'a catastrophic slide'. Only a decade after that same department had encouraged its construction and presented the project with an award, it concluded: 'At best the local authority can hope to make it tolerable for the next decade or so, but eventually because the estate is so monolithic and comprises such a large proportion of their housing, the possibility of demolition is one that will have to be considered.'

Architects' angst

Such was the pressure on architects to comment that the RIBA's president, Larry Rolland, sought to draw fire from the borough architect responsible. In a statement he focused on what he called 'Haringey Council's dangerous policy of using the estate as a gathering ground for problem tenants'. He continued:

> The ghetto-like atmosphere, where only 10 per cent of the tenants paid full rent, is the basic cause of problems on the estate. The council cannot collect enough money to pay the rents, so how can it maintain the building?
>
> Faced with such a low income from the estate it is understandable that the rate-capped borough fails to meet its obligations in terms of capital resources to put back into the estate.

He criticized the neglected landscaping, and argued that if both this and the building itself had been well maintained the estate would have survived intact.

The appraisal failed to pay attention to poor finish during construction, or to comment on building techniques. The residents' point of view was barely considered. However, one final paragraph sparked off some of the most lively and outspoken exchanges the profession had seen for years: 'Given the standards of maintenance and security in such an urban community as the Barbican, it is plain that these standards could and should be applied to similarly high-density developments as Broadwater Farm.' That statement was incredibly naive, because the Barbican had been designed as a complex composed entirely of privately owned flats, each of which faced high service charges for maintenance. If councils were to impose such standards, rents would soar.

I had visited Broadwater Farm; the buildings looked decayed

and neglected. I instantly sympathized with the tenants. Poor design had undoubtedly contributed to such strong disaffection. The layouts of the public areas were unwelcoming, the concrete was stained and unpleasant-looking, and there was little in the landscaping to alleviate the overpowering ugliness. The atmosphere was overwhelmingly alien.

Rolland's comments provoked considerable press attention and one architect, Jim Sneddon, replied in the 25 October 1985 issue of *Building Design* with an account of his two-year experience as a young, relatively low-paid member of his profession living at Broadwater Farm:

Even with the most elastic imagination Broadwater Farm cannot be considered good housing. Denial that poor housing is a major element of people's anger about the world in which they live is dishonest. Yet I heard both of these comments as architects turned and fled from the Broadwater Farm tenants' condemnation of the design of their estate.

I would suggest that the design set the users and managers impossible tasks for maintenance and security. For architects to blame the managers is akin to throwing someone overboard and saying they drowned because they couldn't swim. Nobody would suggest that bad architecture causes riots, at least not yet, but in the case of Broadwater Farm it has meant years of misery for thousands of people.

The architectural dreams of the thirties have become the nightmare of the seventies and eighties. Time has shown the confidence of the sixties to be an unbelievable arrogance on the part of the architectural profession. If it seeks to win back any credibility and to have a useful place in our society, it must accept that twenty years ago, seduced by Modernist manifestos, it frequently failed to meet the challenge of mass public housing. Quantity not quality was demanded by politicians, and that is precisely what they received, helped along by self-interested industrialists who were the only winners in all this.

With the present revival of interest in the Modern Movement [he was probably referring to occasional quotes in the press from leading Modernists such as Denys Lasdun] Broadwater Farm comes as a timely reminder of the human costs of architects being mesmerized by stylistic considerations, and the design concept becoming separated from the realities of life.

I should like to make it clear that I do not consider Broadwater Farm to be the worst in Britain; there are many more where the catalogue of ills would make those [of Broadwater Farm] seem insignificant. The estate is sadly only unique in that a riot has briefly focused attention on the inadequacies of mass public housing schemes built in a rush to supply the maximum amount of housing to satisfy political need. By living on the estate for more than two years I was able to appreciate first hand how people's lives could be drastically affected by decisions taken by architects.

At the end of November another article appeared in *Building Design*, this time from the RIBA's new public affairs director, David Attwell. He had fed Rolland with much of the background information for the RIBA's initial response to the riot. Under the headline 'What's Wrong with Broadwater Farm?' Attwell said he had visited the estate to see the problems for himself. His final comments pushed the architectural debate into the national press:

It was instructive to see who was actually moving around the estate on the morning I was there. There were plenty of mums and kids, but almost all the males I saw emerging from the flats were Rastafarians. They then apparently formed the hardcore of the unemployed and I was given to understand that it was the police clamping down on their drug dealing that was the primary cause of the riots. It is a tragedy that the Rastafarians, with their drug-orientated culture and messages of resentment, despair, conflict and confrontation, have become a symbol of the current problems. Martyrdom is what they seek, and they

are an entirely unrepresentative mass of Caribbean communities in Britain.

The press thoroughly revelled in the professional infighting and
criticized the RIBA for its reactions. Replying to an item in the
Guardian, Rolland, now blaming the buildings themselves rather
than their lack of maintenance, said:

All Broadwater Farm needed was a bit of love and care. The real
problem has been the same throughout Broadwater Farm's
miserable existence – it was built, like most giant system-built
housing schemes at the time, too fast and too cheaply. Nye
Bevan, great man of the people though he was, only made
himself unpopular politically in the fifties when he called for
30,000 quality council-built homes a year rather than skimping
in quality and trying to produce 300,000 or more, as all
governments felt they had to do until the severe economic
depression set in in the mid-seventies. As long as governments
and local authorities expect to get architecture on the cheap,
they can safely forget the idea of decent, well looked after
housing schemes.

Incensed by the lack of consistency in Rolland's remarks,
criticism then came from the RIBA's Community Architecture
Group and its chairman Ian Finlay, who demanded that the
president consult the group before issuing any more statements
on Broadwater Farm. Another group member, Ben Derbyshire,
said: 'It is extremely worrying that the simplistic argument which
has gone through the press is that community initiatives don't
work. The group wants the RIBA to assemble evidence from
architects and others working in riot-prone areas and draw up a
more considered response.'
This call coincided with the report I was preparing, with
contributions from others, including the Prince of Wales's Royal
Jubilee Trust director, Harold Hayward, on the background to the

riots in the Handsworth district of Birmingham. The Prince had wanted to know how community architecture could help improve inner city housing. Both Hayward and I welcomed the community group's initiative and hoped to incorporate the RIBA's findings in our own report, which was to be submitted to the Prince before Christmas.

Divided Britain

The Broadwater Farm debate coincided with another furore in the press over inner cities, when a banner headline appeared in the *Manchester Evening News* on 23 October declaring an exclusive from Prince Charles: 'My Fear for the Future'. This was the start of what soon became known as the 'Divided Britain' story.

I had recently had dinner with Prince Charles aboard the royal train in the south of England, to continue our discussions on inner city problems. I had taken with me a series of slides illustrating refurbishment projects to show the Prince. Peter Sharples, a reporter on the *Manchester Evening News*, had somehow heard about the meeting and rang to find out what had been said. What I told him were my thoughts on the inner cities and on how I would solve their problems. The next day, to my complete surprise, splashed right across the front of the *Manchester Evening News* was a photograph of the Prince and me. The story began: 'The biggest fear of Prince Charles is that he will inherit the throne of a divided Britain. This is revealed exclusively along with the future king's own efforts to find answers to the riots and mayhem in the inner cities.'

This story was directly related to national fears that there would be more riots on the scale of Broadwater Farm. The press knew that any comments from Prince Charles, already outspoken in his social concern, would make the headlines:

Charles has formed his own 'think tank' to come up with ideas.

He has asked researchers to get to the heart of the problem in Handsworth, Brixton, Toxteth, as well as Moss Side. His aim is to change the attitude of the black minorities who fear they have no future in communities of high unemployment and mounting drug addiction. According to his advisers, the Prince is prepared to force his way through parliamentary red tape to ensure that his country is not split into fractions of the 'haves' and 'have nots'.

Then followed an account of my own feelings about Britain's inner city problems, which read as if they belonged to Prince Charles. I had spoken about potential no-go areas in cities, the fact that the country had apparently learned little from the lessons of four years before with the riots of 1981, and that community architecture could breathe new life into run-down areas. It was all regurgitated as the Prince of Wales's thoughts.

By the afternoon of the same day the story was picked up by the *London Standard* and again splashed right across the entire front page. That evening news bulletins featured the *Manchester Evening News* front page, and the following morning every national paper ran the story.

I was described as the most wanted man in Fleet Street, but curiously none of the papers telephoned me before they ran their front page stories based on the *Manchester Evening News* report. However, the next day my home and office were besieged by reporters. My staff was grilled – even about such trivial things as what food I liked and what clothes I wore.

The Prince of Wales was in Australia at the time. But that didn't stop the *Sun* publishing a story saying we had argued over my 'betrayal' of his confidence and that we were no longer on speaking terms. The Prince ignored this embroidery of fact. The story was not even mentioned when we met shortly afterwards at one of the Kensington Palace dinners I had organized. The saga continued for almost two weeks until a major story broke in Cyprus. My life and that of my office in Macclesfield returned to normal.

Despite the distortion of facts, and considerable personal disruption, the media coverage did have some beneficial effects. Inner city decay and its damaging effects on people's lives received a welcome boost of attention. Buckingham Palace agreed that some of the sentiments expressed werre those of Prince Charles, and he rapidly became championed as the people's hero. Although clearly in no position to be drawn into a political row, he represented exactly what many people believed.

As a result of fresh media concern spurred on by Prince Charles, the RIBA and representatives from the construction industry lobbied government for more action in the inner cities. The Decaying Britain campaign was launched by the RIBA to highlight the rotten condition of urban areas.

Also in 1985 the Institute, in partnership with the *Times*, set up the Community Enterprise Scheme Awards to boost self-help projects. And to make advice more easily available, a community architecture resource centre was founded at the RIBA's London headquarters in Portland Place.

By the end of the year the construction boom was well underway. Docklands was enjoying massive injections of private money, the Lloyd's Building was nearing completion – its designer, Richard Rogers, scooped the Royal Gold Medal for Architecture – and plans were submitted for the vast Broadgate development project by London's Liverpool Street Station. The heavily criticized designs for both the National Gallery extension and Mies van der Rohe's tower at Mansion House Square – the 'carbuncle' and the 'glass stump' – were both rejected.

Faith in the City

At the end of 1985, the five years of critical reports and speeches continued with an unprecedented attack from religious leaders. The Church of England joined in with its *Faith in the City* report. The

400-page document had been commissioned by the Archbishop of Canterbury, Dr Robert Runcie, and had taken his team two years to research. The commission's chairman was Sir Richard O'Brien, former chairman of the Manpower Services Commission, and acting as secretary was John Pearson from the DoE. It was the most comprehensive study ever prepared by the Church on social and economic conditions in modern times.

The report was due for public release on 3 December. But after copies had been delivered to the government the document was leaked to the press a week early, effectively destroying its impact – much to the annoyance of the Church. Relations between No. 10 and Dr Runcie had been strained for some time, since his statement declaring that government shortcomings compelled the Church of England to act as the conscience of the nation and oppose any economic policies which were unjust and damaging to national unity. Calling it an attack upon Conservatism, by the time *Faith in the City* was officially published it had been branded by the government as Marxist.

It was a hard-hitting attack on the government's dogmatic and inflexible approach to inner city decay. Its authors observed that too much emphasis was placed on the individual at the expense of communities and demanded that more money be spent on inner cities. It even suggested that the public would be prepared to pay higher taxes to guarantee national stability as well as to secure a better deal for the poor in urban areas. There were calls for changes in mortgage tax relief on the grounds that home owners, the better-off, were being subsidized at the expense of council tenants. And it wanted increased rate support grants for local authorities. Youth unemployment was identified as a major issue, and there were demands for positive discrimination in helping racial minorities.

The report was debated in the House of Commons and provided the government with an ideal opportunity to announce a string of spending figures to counter the criticism. The Conservatives claimed that spending on the Urban Programme had doubled since 1979 to £338 million, that its grants to reclaim derelict land had also doubled, and that support for the voluntary sector had trebled. Private sector investment was also held up as a success. The £77 million spent by government on urban development grants had reaped £330 million from private investors, which the Conservatives claimed would not have been forthcoming if they had not triggered it off with their own contribution.

The reality, as I well knew, was that the programme had ground to a halt. In real terms the spending for 1985–6 was less than that for 1982–3. The cash given through the Urban Programme with one hand was taken back through cuts with the other. In 1981–2 local councils had received (at 1985 prices) £2 billion in rate support, but in 1985–6 that figure had been slashed to £1.5 billion. The amount lost in rate support was ten times that gained from the Urban Programme.

The Church report was excellent, even if it showed a certain naivety in its financial analysis. The government was expert at defending itself with figures, and it was clear that any future reports would have to employ superior financial advisers if they were to win at that game. The government also tried to discredit the report by alleging that it was blatantly anti-Conservative. They cited the fact that the chairman was a former member of the Labour Party, and that other members of the Church commission involved in the investigations included union representatives.

The recommendations disappeared in the smokescreen of accusation and counter-accusation. However, one tangible benefit was that the Church set up a £2 million Urban Fund. And despite its rigorous defence, the government was once again under national pressure to come up with real results.

7 Sound and Fury

Throughout the spring and summer of 1986 the Tories made repeated assurances that their policies for regeneration were working. We were told that the economy had made a strong recovery, that unemployment was falling, that there was continued effort to create jobs and that the inner cities were to receive more help. There was a deluge of new urban initiatives, and the Urban Programme was stepped up to £494 million for 1986–7 – an increase of £14 million over the previous year.

The latest regeneration packages included the founding of five City Action Teams involving representatives from the departments of the Environment, Trade and Industry, and Employment. Their brief was to work closely with local authorities, the private and voluntary sectors, and set up employment, training and self-help schemes in Liverpool, Birmingham, Manchester, Newcastle and the London Boroughs of Hackney, Islington and Lambeth. In addition, a further eight pilot sites had been targeted for the Inner Cities Task Force to tackle unemployment and disadvantage faced by people, particularly the young, in urban areas.

Following the lead set by London Docklands and Merseyside, four new Urban Development Corporations were designated at Trafford Park, Manchester; on Teesside; in the Black Country; and in Tyne and Wear. Each had a budget of between £100 million and £160 million to spend over six years. Most of it was to be used for reclaiming derelict or disused land.

In housing, Estate Action replaced the DoE's Urban Housing Renewal Unit. Its tasks included tackling homelessness by encouraging councils to bring empty property back into use and to improve run-down estates. Almost ninety schemes were approved in 1986, involving £31.5 million of government spending on 45,000 homes.

Package deals

The government, with help from image-makers Saatchi and Saatchi, had formulated a slick, glossy approach to tackling the inner cities, designed specifically to appeal to private investors. Urban renewal was wrapped up and presented as a marketing exercise. But despite all the talk and promises, the root problems of improving poor housing remained untouched.

Many local authorities had boosted their incomes through the sale of council houses. However, they were not free to spend that money. Central government, with its eyes on controlling inflation, allowed the release of just 20 per cent of the newly accumulated cash. The remaining 80 per cent was banked, to be used in spending programmes spread over subsequent years.

But even here the initiatives were misdirected. They profited the richer, usually Conservative-controlled authorities which had been promoting sales. Tenants could afford to buy, and the property was usually in better condition because more money had been available for maintenance. The poorer councils struggled under the burden of cuts and increasing maintenance demanded on their deteriorating estates – in the bitter knowledge that millions of pounds of council money lay out of reach in banks.

The Conservatives continued their policy of boosting the economy through the creation of new jobs. They also hoped that reduced provision of council housing would be balanced by the encouragement of private developers. The flaw was that, while this worked in a few selected areas, developers found it much easier and more profitable to develop outside city centres.

A report fit for a Prince

Prince Charles once more took a lead. He asked me to organize a dinner at Kensington Palace for a number of architects, industrialists and financial, community and planning experts to discuss compiling an inner cities survey. It was to outline our ideas for a comprehensive regeneration programme, including housing and proposals for disused buildings, together with the creation of jobs. The document was to be published in 1987 as the RIBA's *Inner Cities* report, and Prince Charles agreed to forward it in person to industrialists and central government.

To prepare the report the RIBA formed an Inner Cities Committee in May 1986. Its members included experts such as Fred Roche, deputy chairman of Conran Roche; David Barker, managing director of Hill Samuel Investment; Philip Chappel, of the Association of Investment Trust Companies; David Couttie, housing development controller of the Halifax Building Society; Robert Davies, development director of Business in the Community; Professor Peter Hall, planning expert; and Jim Sneddon of CAWG. The high-calibre committee drew together advisers competent to tackle the complexities of design and planning, finance, housing and community needs. My job was to act as co-ordinator, to ensure the brief was followed and to report on progress to Prince Charles.

Party piece

During the autumn run-up to the general election I was invited to speak at each of the four main party conferences. Urban problems were key issues on every agenda. I described the appalling extent of housing problems and suggested to each conference that the only way out of the mess was to introduce the type of governmental changes earlier suggested by Michael Heseltine and Lord Scarman. I also attacked the folly of the existing piecemeal approach, with seven different departments — Employment, Environment, Trade and Industry, Health and Social Security,

Transport, the Home Office and the Treasury – individually contributing help to the urban areas. Britain needed one co-ordinated agency composed of the best brains from each ministry.

To illustrate how such simple changes could produce highly successful results I cited the recent Mexican earthquake disaster; faced with an environment in ruins and around forty thousand homeless families, the government rapidly dismantled its rigid system and formed an emergency committee to tackle repairs and building. I saw the British tragedy of homelessness and poor housing as a not dissimilar disaster. Although it had happened slowly, it was on a much larger scale.

I described the decline of whole areas such as Merseyside, West Yorkshire, the North-East and parts of Scotland, Wales and Northern Ireland, where unemployment was then running at more than 50 per cent above the national average and where children were growing up with no expectation of having a real job. The most able had left home, draining areas of skilled labour and further exacerbating the divide between rich and poor. The results had been shown to us all in the riots, but no successful attempts had since been made to repair the damage. Even such expensive projects as the Liverpool Garden Festival, although well intentioned, had caused alienation and mistrust.

An injection of money was not enough to solve the problems. A new way of thinking had to be adopted to encourage people to help themselves. The dependency culture had to be broken – starting with community-run housing schemes tapping the resources of the unemployed and preventing the inevitability of violent change.

The speeches were well received by each party. But I suppose I knew that, even if the ideas were to be wrapped up as part of an electoral package, it would be some time before I would see them put into practice.

Shaken and stirred

The summer of 1986 also saw the RIBA in the throes of an election battle. The official statement on the Broadwater Farm riots had stirred up considerable resentment within a large section of the membership. They had displayed an arrogant disinterest and had been loath to accept criticism or admit that the design might have been at fault.

This determination to avoid confronting reality, not just at Broadwater Farm but in poor design elsewhere, was infuriating. Having been involved in the politics of the architectural profession throughout the previous ten years, I saw how outmoded the thinking had become. I had become bitterly disillusioned with the way the RIBA was running its affairs.

My patience eventually ran out during one particular debate, held in May, on reducing the numbers of architects coming into the profession and closing architectural schools. This showed just how far out of touch the RIBA was with current demands. I resolved to try and make changes. For some time I had been arguing that there were too *few* architects in Britain. Even during the recession only 2 per cent had been out of work, and, as we appeared to be entering a boom period, it seemed ridiculous to talk about reducing the number. It was one of the most important debates ever held in the council chamber, but to my dismay only thirty-six of the sixty-two elected members turned up to take part.

Ever since Lord Esher had been president in the sixties, the RIBA's council had treated the education debate with tremendous gravity. The government had made it clear it wanted cut-backs in the numbers of student places, but I couldn't believe that our professional body was kow-towing to those wishes. The council drew up its hit list for closure – the Huddersfield School in Yorkshire, the North East Polytechnic in London and the Belfast School were all threatened. The two Edinburgh schools were instructed to merge. The policy seemed to dictate that, where there was a polytechnic and a university school in the same town, one would be forced to close. A special general meeting on education was held, and again most council members failed to attend. Did nobody care?

My frustration made me realize that if I was to have a voice at all I would have to stand for the presidency. I drew up my manifesto and showed it to a few friends to gauge their response. I criticized the Institute for drifting under poor leadership, and said that no amount of marketing bluff would conceal its gross inadequacies. Proposals for these education cuts presented the profession with the most substantial threat for 152 years, and yet a discreet silence was being maintained. Research and excellence in design were being ignored, and the regions were suffering from financial starvation. There was clearly a desperate need for a radical new approach.

The support I received was enthusiastic and came from all quarters – Sir Hugh Casson; Keith Scott, head of Britain's biggest architectural firm, the Building Design Partnership; Bill Reed, head of Britain's largest public sector architect's office in Birmingham; Ben Derbyshire of Hunt Thompson Associates; Professor Riley of Nottingham University; Richard Rogers; and Norman Foster. It was with this sort of backing that I put my name forward as a presidential candidate.

My opponent was Raymond Andrews, who, through the RIBA's creaking old system, was due for his 'turn'. The challenge had only been tried once before: six years previously, Owen Luder had successfully managed to overturn the RIBA's choice of candidate. However, a bitter battle had ensued.

By October the press had taken up the story and, although I was the outside candidate, I was widely tipped as the favourite. I wanted a shake-up at the RIBA: to draw up firm policy ideas, get rid of complacency, stop the education cuts, disband the in-effectual Group of Eight building lobby, devolve more power to the regions, support community architecture and professional excellence, and provide stronger, more capable management at the

Institute. In order to win, as in any election campaign, I had to make speeches to the electorate all round the country.

Spare the Rod

Raymond Andrews was a tough opponent. He used the machinery of the RIBA to run his campaign and had the backing of senior staff.

The outgoing president, Larry Rolland, made his own position as an Andrews supporter quite clear. He used the press to make a statement describing my challenge as 'damaging nonsense'. He also refused my request to enlist the participation of the Electoral Reform Society to oversee voting procedure. I was fighting not just a political opponent, but also the entire system backed by the RIBA's machinery.

Andrews fought hard, and launched a personal attack on me in the 7 November issue of *Building* magazine. He argued that I should be dropped as unofficial adviser to Prince Charles. The Prince had spoken out against the house building industry for paying insufficient attention to the problems of dereliction in the inner cities, and Andrews assumed I had been instrumental in forming the Prince's opinions. He said:

> the Prince should choose someone with a wider knowledge and fuller understanding of the profession. Hackney's specialized field of community architecture is only one aspect of inner city renewal and architecture.
>
> Architecture covers a wide range of building types and requires a thorough understanding of both the public and private sectors at national and local levels. Hackney's narrow experience does not accord with the Royal Family's usual standard of taking broad advice.

I was puzzled by Andrews' approach – it seemed out of character, and I suspected he was being influenced by some of the RIBA's old guard.

We rarely met during the campaign, but he did agree to take part in a debate at the Welsh National Opera in Cardiff in November. Here he continued the slanging match, likening me to Arthur Scargill and Derek Hatton. 'If Hackney rocks the boat,' he said, 'he'll rock it too hard and it could go over.' He added, looking directly at me, that 'ambition is the last refuge of failure'. And then my opponent described me as cynical, callous and a charlatan.

The vitriol won him few friends, and the professional press, including *Architects' Journal* and *Building Design*, all came out in my favour. Even *Private Eye* chimed in, with its Nooks and Corners column proclaiming 'Vote Hackney':

Non-architects might assume that Dr Hackney of Macclesfield, the notorious community architect and garrulous unofficial adviser to the Prince of Wales, was a figment of *Private Eye*'s diseased imagination. He is in fact real and he is challenging the favourite Mr Raymond Andrews. If Mr Hackney wins, there is a remote chance that he might bring an end to the years of ruthless philistinism which began when Owen 'sod you' Luder became president after another hotly contested election.

Hackney's personal defects have been much commented on by Raymond Andrews. Now I know nothing damaging about Mr Andrews – he seems to be just boring and mediocre, so the perfect person to continue the institute's disastrous policies.

So, for a faint hope that the decline of the RIBA and thus the much-abused and misunderstood mother of the arts, architecture, can be halted, vote for Rod.

The Andrews camp continued its attacks throughout the campaign, but after the largest-ever recorded poll I was elected president with a majority of 1500 in the late autumn of 1986.

Talking point

At the same time as the RIBA election I was also involved in helping to run and act as president of, the first International Building Communities Conference. Held in November 1986 at London's Astoria Hotel, it was devised to make some sense of the tangle of initiatives on offer to community groups. It also brought together experts working on inner city problems around the world. Over a thousand people attended, all of them sharing the belief that the voluntary sector and communities held the key to renovation.

Speakers included representatives from all the political parties, including Michael Heseltine and Shirley Williams, the building and environmental professions, the Church and the Prince of Wales. The conference also provided the launching pad for two new funds – the Inner City Trust, with Prince Charles as its patron, offering cash and expertise to self-help community groups; and the National Community Aid Fund, set up to help community groups employ professional advisers.

The conference chairman was Lord Scarman, who was by this time one of the foremost champions of the community approach. He spoke out in praise of the efforts made by the public, private and voluntary agencies to breathe new life into inner cities, and stressed the need for an even wider recognition of the grass roots approach.

I really don't like saying 'I told you so', but I did say in the Brixton report that a 'top-down' approach to regeneration of the depressed urban areas had not worked; and I emphasized that people who live in the inner city needed more say and control over their living conditions, over local projects and particularly over the development of their housing. I suggest that people's choice and people's control need to become the keynotes of the debate.

Prince Charles, in his address, openly described his anxieties about urban deprivation; having visited some of my schemes, including Black Road, he fully endorsed the value of human potential:

> Before I had ever heard of community architecture I kept wondering to myself how the situation could be improved and transformed. When I discovered what had been achieved by some remarkable architects working closely with groups of people in run-down parts of our inner cities and towns, the first thing I wanted to do was to see for myself what was actually going on. Having seen several projects and having met the people concerned, who had been involved in either renovating or building their houses, I came away totally enthused by the atmosphere I encountered and by the transformation that had clearly taken place in the lives of individuals and families.
>
> One of the main reasons I believe that the community architecture approach makes sense is because I believe in the individual uniqueness of every human being. Every individual has a contribution to make and a potential to achieve this, if it can be brought out. I believe individuals tend to operate best within a community of other individuals; within an environment that is based on a human scale and which is designed to create a sense of belonging rather than of alienation and anonymity.

All the speakers were highly respected in their particular walks of life, and it was reassuring to recognize that at last our ideas were no longer being dismissed as cranky or fringe. There were even signs that some key members of the Conservative Party had grasped the gravity of the problems. Housing Minister John Patten identified major problems in council estates and supported the future need for more tenant involvement in housing:

> Problems in the inner cities and outer cities have reached a crisis of confidence. I think the estates were really wrong

because they provided the wrong sort of environment. They don't provide homes in which people can feel proud to live. They were designed and built, and, very often since, they have been managed without regard for the desires and preferences of the most important group – the people who live in these homes.

Michael Heseltine also made a powerful speech about his hopes for the future, based on his experiences in Merseyside:

At no time has the interest in the stress areas of inner cities been more intense.

In order to create communities that are a mix of talent, age and independence it is essential to make the cities places where the strong, the more prosperous, the skilled worker, the entrepreneur and vocationally dedicated will choose to live, will choose to work and will choose to invest.

Good doctors, good teachers, good priests, skilled managers, successful entrepreneurs – they all have a role to play in a balanced society, and we have to create an urban environment that competes with the attractions of rural and southern England.

The political approach which emerges from this analysis is clear. First a national recognition that we must build again an urban environment which attracts and does not repel, that is competitive in the market place of human choice, that is not just relevant for those with no choice, but is equally relevant for those with real choice. This government, in my view, has shown in London and Liverpool and in a score of other cities how that process can begin to work.

Secondly, an understanding that to gain a commitment from communities we wish to encourage we must create an atmosphere of local decision, individual enterprise and initiatives supported by a high quality of public service.

The central recognition for progress is that the incentives

must come from government. The nature of the existing dereliction, the inhibiting element of negative land values, and the scale that is necessary to instil confidence in the private sector can only be addressed by a combination of central and local government processes.

The conference was a huge success and attracted excellent media coverage. I felt greatly encouraged by the volume of support, but I was still worried that there was a long way to go before many of the urgent problems could be tackled.

Building condemned

Throughout the spring of 1987 work was being completed on the RIBA's Inner Cities Committee report, which had been inspired by the Prince of Wales. It fulfilled the brief of providing an analysis of the scale of the urban disaster together with making a range of constructive proposals for revival. Released in May, it was sent to all MPs during the run-up to the June election.

The urban debate was a central issue that no party could afford to ignore. The findings of a range of reports, including the RIBA's, confirmed that living conditions and employment prospects for the worst-off had seen little improvement during Margaret Thatcher's eight-year term. With my particular interest in housing I knew, for example, that the backlog of repairs to council housing was estimated to be growing at a rate of £900 million annually – Birmingham alone, continuing at its 1987 rate of progress, would have needed a staggering six hundred years to carry out a full housing modernization programme; homelessness had doubled since 1979 to around 100,000 and yet some 112,000 council houses and flats and 545,000 private homes lay empty in England; and 100,000 acres of land lay derelict in the inner cities. The figures were extremely depressing.

The RIBA report identified inner city decay as 'one of the most serious crises confronting Britain'. It continued with a hard-hitting attack on the failure to resolve problems and concluded with what I consider to be the key recommendation – that a central funding agency should be formed:

The insidious, cumulative effect of an array of unresolved social, economic and environmental problems that have developed over the last thirty years now presents a direct threat to the quality of urban life and civil peace.

Decaying housing, industrial dereliction at the heart of once thriving urban areas, declining investment, high unemployment, poverty and social deprivation, all bear testimony to the severity and complexity of the urban crisis and the necessity for direct and urgent action.

Few informed observers believe that there is any quick or cheap solution, but most would endorse the judgement of those individuals and organizations active in the field who believe that the conquest of inner city decay will bring rewards commensurate with the sustained effort that is necessary. A strategy for carrying out this task forms the core of our proposal. Nothing is more corrosive of successful action than the combination of delay, inaccessible resources and official indifference that has so often confronted it in the past. Want of attention, as well as inadequate investment and support from central government, can starve local endeavour and foster dissatisfaction and despair. For this reason we recommend as a matter of urgency the formation of a powerful financial and institutional infrastructure to co-ordinate and administer long-term support for local enterprise. In our view the best way to provide this infrastructure is through the creation of a National Urban Renewal Agency responsible to the Secretary of State for the Environment and charged with raising and administering large-scale public and private sector investment for inner city regeneration.

All for one and one for all

The agency proposal was something in which I had great faith. The Conservative government had shown no signs of forming a powerful inner city committee, and so I saw NURA as the chance to co-ordinate funding at the very least.

NURA was to work as a centralized pool of money and expertise. In 1987 around £500 million of public money was being spent through the Urban Programme, Urban Development Grants, Urban Regeneration Grants, Derelict Land Grants and the new generation of Urban Development Corporations. NURA would be made responsible for those, along with a further public fund investment of £500,000. Companies offering money would be offered American-style tax incentives: if their annual profits amounted to £10 million and they donated £2 million of them, they would simply be taxed on the remaining £8 million.

The £1 billion 'pool' would then be used to attract £4 billion from private investors. Where, for example, they were prepared to contribute the majority of a project's cost, NURA would make up the balance. Total annual regeneration investment could reach some £5 billion.

A typical scheme would involve a private developer buying and renovating a council tower block for £2 million. Around £400,000 would be offered by NURA in the form of either a grant or a loan. In exchange for a grant NURA would exercise some control over the future management of the block and would claim a portion of the income in rents or sales. The financing was devised to be flexible enough to offer similar renovation packages for buildings as varied as shops, warehouses and factories.

The report was circulated by Prince Charles to industry chiefs and to the Prime Minister. Several industrialists supported the ideas, but the government made no reaction. Although the report was eventually shelved, it continues to stand as a useful framework for revitalizing neglected areas and buildings.

'Now the inner cities'

Margaret Thatcher's pledge to help the inner cities was swiftly endorsed when she returned to power for a third term in June 1987. At 3 a.m. in her victory speech she summarized her successes in boosting the economy and thus generating jobs, and then made her famous promise: 'Now the inner cities.' Perhaps, at last, we would see some action.

True to her word, the Economic Urban Policy group was founded as part of the Cabinet's Economic Strategy Committee. Formed along similar lines to those I had suggested years before, it was composed of members from the major government departments who were to co-ordinate all initiatives. The government was not keen to see any further violent manifestations of unrest. Mrs Thatcher was to chair the group, which had as its leading lights Nicholas Ridley from the DoE and Lord Young from the DTI. After announcing her chairmanship the Prime Minister was quoted as saying: 'I have taken over and there may be the need to bang a few heads together. One of the main things is to get the co-operation between departments.'

But it was hopeless from the start. Although Ridley and Young both called themselves Thatcherites, each had a totally different approach to the cities. Ridley was attracted to free enterprise and urban aesthetics, while Young was more interested in the challenge of creating jobs. Two more different people could not have been chosen to try to establish a co-ordinated approach. All ministries wanted the kudos of repairing damaged urban areas, and so rivalry continued to persist. It was also evident that Thatcher was reluctant to channel more government money into deprived areas and that, by her absence even at the group's first meeting, she clearly couldn't invest the required energy, enthusiasm or commitment to make things work.

One of the main contributions from the group, however, was the Action for Cities programme. Launched nine months later, in the spring of 1988, to co-ordinate the DoE's £500 million inner cities spending, it was devised with the express purpose of helping the poor share in the new prosperity.

Breaking the mould

While the first drafts of the government's programme were being made, I took up my post as president of the RIBA on the World Day of Architecture, 1 July 1987. It was probably twenty years since a non-Modernist had held the post. Architects had been receiving a bad press for several years and so I set out to improve public perception of the profession, to increase the exchange between designers, clients and the public, and to turn the beautiful 1930s' headquarters into an architectural centre.

Having discovered that the Institute faced debts of around £1 million, I called in management consultants to identify the major financial problems. The results showed that the thirteen regions needed strengthening through the injection of more cash; staff appointments, however, had to be cut back, the loss-making *RIBA Journal* needed reorganization, and the governing council was to be reduced in size so as to become more effective. I appointed Bill Rodgers, the former Labour Party Secretary of State for Transport and one of the so-called 'Gang of Four', as director general. His arrival at the RIBA was the result of a recommendation from the management consultants, and with his political and managerial skills and experience he was an ideal choice.

My avowed intention of raising the professional image of the RIBA involved me in a steady stream of TV appearances and radio broadcasts, ambassadorial dinners, political and trade conferences, and meetings with MPs. I felt it was essential to build a high profile during the first twelve months of my two-year presidency so as to publicize the change of approach. I also needed to establish as many and as wide a range of contacts as possible to ensure a constant flow and exchange of ideas between professions, countries and government departments.

Coinciding with the country's economic boom, the construction industry now saw an upturn. Architects were back in demand, and so I successfully helped to quash government plans to reduce the number of training places. Given the volume of new building work I considered it imperative to avoid the mistakes made in the boom years of the sixties, and so the RIBA council under my chairmanship, introduced compulsory training courses to ensure that practising architects kept abreast of new legislation and the latest research into building materials. It was especially pertinent in view of the new wave of building disasters which had come to light.

Although structures were not collapsing as they had done twenty years previously, an altogether more insidious range of problems had arisen with the spread of legionnaire's disease through modern air-conditioning systems. The USA had also identified Sick Building Syndrome as a hazard of working in newly built offices: workers complained of nausea, dizziness, sore throats and skin rashes which mysteriously cleared up at weekends. One American employee successfully sued two hundred defendants including an architect, a building contractor, a ventilation engineer and manufacturers of products such as floor tiles, glue and carpets; he claimed that his health had been injured by the polluted air in which he worked. Damages of $700,000 were agreed. The World Health Organization also declared that 'sealed' buildings — those with fixed windows and a mechanically controlled airflow — were hazardous, forcing their occupants to breathe in each other's germs, fumes, pesticides and moulds.

With renewed media attention focused on design faults, there were yet more changes perceptible within the profession. A great deal had been learned throughout the sixties and seventies, and many architects had acquired a more responsible attitude to design after realizing that they could not ignore its users. It was also a change partly imposed by the shrinkage of public sector contracts and the growth of the private sector, in which demand was market-led. With both their reputations and their livelihood at stake, combined with the fact that designers were in such great demand, increasing numbers of architects took the bold step of refusing to work on projects if the clients responsible were demanding a quick, cheap product.

There were also signs that training was changing – again market-led. Since renovation and the reuse of old buildings were now providing between 30 and 50 per cent of the workload, architects needed to understand the vitality of old buildings, to know how they were made, how they could be adapted, how the materials were used and how they could be recycled. Up until the late seventies all a Modernist architect needed to know about old buildings was that, once demolished, they could be used for hardcore. And so, instead of teaching traditional building methods as if they were history, the subject had a new, practical, contemporary application. But the changes were sure to be slow because tutors were Modernist-trained, and, while Modernism as a style was no longer being taught, its élitist detachment remained a potent mythology. However, students themselves have brought pressure to bear on the way they are taught and have now become a great deal more questioning.

Home help

A shift away from the mass building policies was also evident in government, and I was invited to advise John Patten at the Home Office on how design could help to eliminate crime from estates. Although fewer than 30,000 council homes a year were being built – 10 per cent of the volume being produced in the sixties – the Conservatives had, rather late in the day, learned something from the errors of the past.

I suggested that they abandon any new building of deck access-style blocks with their dark corners and vulnerable spaces. I pointed out, too, that towers had major drawbacks such as underground car parks, dangerous lifts and plenty of hiding places. Outside spaces with no clear ownership also made it impossible to tell whether people passing through were tenants, visitors or intruders. I also stressed the need for a return to the old street systems which allowed people the chance to know who their neighbours were, to foster community spirit, and to draw up on open ground clear demarcation lines between public and private areas. These ideas were indisputably old-fashioned, but they had worked for a very long time and I could see no reason why they shouldn't work again.

I was also called in to advise William Waldegrave at the Department of the Environment. He had read the RIBA's *Inner Cities* report and was concerned about the dilapidation of council estates. The received opinion at the DoE was that the estates simply needed minor maintenance to make them attractive and habitable. Private sector investors had been invited into a number of local authorities and been offered blocks for nominal sums, but it was already becoming clear that take-up was slow – many investment companies had tested the market and realized the extent of the problems. Waldegrave had no figures to show the extent of the decay, and he was keen to identify the degree of remedial work necessary to bring properties up to a reasonable standard. This was to be the start of the Housing Action Trusts scheme (HATS).

I suggested that surveys should be undertaken at three of the country's worst-condition estates – Hulme in Manchester, Hyde Park in Sheffield and Broadwater Farm in Tottenham. Eventually, however, six different sites were chosen – in Leeds, Sandwell, Southwark, Lambeth, Tower Hamlets and Sunderland – for political reasons, so as to downplay the acute crisis. They were in a far better condition than those I had identified. But, even so, the survey results came as an unpleasant surprise for government: each flat required an average expenditure of around £35,000 on essential repairs.

A fund of £190 million had been set aside by the DoE for the six HATS areas, but it became evident that at least three times that amount would be needed if the recommendations and figures were accepted. After extending the HATS findings to all estates, the bill for repairing state housing nationwide exceeded £200 billion. The government now faced a housing problem far greater than it had been since World War II. Forty years of effort had been virtually wasted. The costs were so enormous that government had little hope of making repairs. Private investors could not be relied on to pick up the bill, and still the role of local people in regenerating their own areas was totally discounted.

Out of control

The private sector, however, did respond to the government-devised free-for-all of London Docklands. This was the jewel in the Conservatives' crown and was being heavily promoted as a key example of how derelict wasteland could be rejuvenated.

The London Docklands Development Corporation was created, along with the Merseyside scheme, immediately after the rioting of 1981. It was founded on the basis that, with minimal government funding and the relaxation of planning controls and regulations, developers could be encouraged into areas previously considered undesirable.

By 1988 land prices had rocketed from as little as £100,000 per acre to £4 million. Housing, leisure, office and shopping complexes had mushroomed, and there were promises that, with the completion of enormous schemes like the £4 billion Canary Wharf with its 800-foot skyscraper centrepiece (criticized for threatening to obscure views of St Paul's), around eighty thousand jobs would be imported into the area.

However, although the publicity sounded impressive the reality was less spectacular. The Docklands Light Railway was suffering technical and capacity problems. Rising land prices were forcing developers to build higher to recoup costs. The roads were inadequate; high mortgage rates slowed down sales, bankrupting builders; the quality of architectural design was lamentable; and local people felt ostracized. The hotch-potch approach and complete lack of co-ordination, combined with the injection of too much money too quickly was as damaging environmentally as the old mass housing programmes.

During one visit there to talk to Tower Hamlets Chamber of Commerce I met a couple who were about to move to Kent. They had lived in the area for many years but had become victims of the boom. The husband was a redundant dockworker; despite his trying for years, there seemed to be no work on the building sites for local men. Both he and his wife spoke about the changes which had affected them: it was no longer possible to buy a pie and a pint in their local pub because it had been invaded by yuppies and turned into a wine bar selling tequila sunrises and pina coladas; the roads were clogged with cars and building lorries; they disliked the 'Toytown' houses springing up around them; and many of their friends had moved away. They were delighted to have been offered just under £200,000 for their small family house, and had decided to join the exodus. But even though they would gain financially they felt they had been forced out of their home.

In complete contrast, the Merseyside scheme had been slow to take off. The framework for regeneration was exactly the same as that used in London, but it had many advantages. The area was considerably smaller. It had a natural focus: the Albert Docks. The development corporation encouraged developers to use the local workforce, and companies like Barratts agreed to build properties at prices well within the reach of Merseysiders. Money was in short supply, which was a blessing. It enforced a well-organized approach which combined steady work on buildings and infra-structure concurrently.

The big boom

The building boom was continuing around the country. Increased national prosperity was promoting housing and commercial development. Home ownership had increased dramatically under the Conservatives, and so increasing numbers of new houses were required to satisfy demand. Small, private housing estates were appearing with monotonous regularity on town fringes.

Those companies thriving under Tory rule had become much more image-conscious and were keen to upgrade their offices and factories. Many built new premises, while others stripped their sixties' and seventies' Modernist buildings of their old fascias and re-clad them with eighties-style smoked or mirrored glass and, of course, a dash of high-tech stainless steel. Britain was also revelling in a retail boom which saw the construction of countless new shopping complexes, out-of-town shopping centres and huge supermarkets. Massive regeneration projects – such as Quinlan Terry's Richmond Riverside, Bristol Docks and Prince's Square in Glasgow – were underway in almost every town and city.

Recent building has encompassed every possible style – homes are largely traditional, but factories, office blocks, shopping centres and regeneration schemes range from neo-Classical through to Post-Modernist and high-tech. But there is a disappointing lack of flair in the design of so many projects; the worst culprits are supermarkets, DIY super-stores and small housing estates, which are all too often churned out to a formula. However, it has been heartening to see companies such as Sainsbury's following a policy of commissioning bold pieces of architecture, like the Ian Pollard designs for its Kensington Homebase (although it is now insisting on modifications to the final building) and Nicholas Grimshaw's supermarket in Camden. Most encouraging of all is the fact that much of the new building work is of a far higher quality than would have been expected a decade ago.

Vision of Britain

At the end of 1988 came a television programme which focused the nation's attention on what was happening to their towns and cities – Prince Charles's *Vision of Britain*. In his characteristic style the Prince boldly criticized what he considered to be the fundamental flaws of environmental design. He attacked the utilitarian and poorly built and praised those schemes, such as Richmond Riverside, which had been devised with some consideration for their surroundings. The views he was voicing were the deeply held ones of a silent majority.

The media swooped on the story. Coverage was extensive, and the architectural and environmental debate hit the headlines once again. Prince Charles was heralded as the people's hero.

At first, I found myself in the position of being one of the few architects who openly stated that they enjoyed the programme. Others, among them many committed Modernists, were affronted and considered the attack to be unwarranted, ill informed and harmful. James Stirling threatened to return his RIBA Gold Medal, while Denys Lasdun was dismayed at the Prince's assault on his National Theatre designs. I later found out that I was far from being alone and quite a lot of lesser-known architects who did not have access to the press had said how much they enjoyed it. In fact, I would go so far as to say that the majority of architects who saw the programme enjoyed it.

The RIBA Council was called to discuss the matter: the atmosphere was fairly relaxed, and we agreed to support the Prince's comments. Modernist purists were, of course, disappointed by the Institute's response, but interestingly their diminished lobbying force did not rally for a vociferous resistance.

Humanism not Modernism

I ceased to be President of RIBA in July 1989. At the end of my two years its appalling financial position had still not been straightened out but at least we were one year ahead of schedule in pulling back the deficit. Otherwise, I managed to steer the RIBA towards Europe to take its part with the eleven other countries in order that by 1992 there could be a free flow of architects working throughout the EEC, and I made sure that the Institute was closely involved with 'green' issues.

Without concentrating on community architecture to the detriment of all else, I would like to think that during my term it came of age and became accepted as one of the normal ways of practising rather than just a ginger group activity.

At the time of writing, the end of the worst excesses of the Modern Movement are in sight. Mass public housing programmes have been stopped. Council housing stocks have dwindled and government is still pursuing a policy of selling off these properties to tenants. Corbusian-style urban planning is being cast aside in favour of the small-scale. Uniform utilitarian styles have been replaced by the more familiar and traditional, and experimentation with new materials is now approached with considerable caution. Mass planning, mass building, mass spending and the presiding, élitist architect are concepts that are dead and buried. The call made by my successor at RIBA, Maxwell Hutchinson, for a new strong single-minded movement of neo-Modernism as we go into the new millenium is really just a smokescreen for the increasing advance of a new pluralism in architecture.

Modernism has been rejected by the majority of the public and will, I feel, only remain a force within the narrow fields of painting and sculpture. In architecture, Modernism has become an embarrassment. And if it should be retained as part of the new pluralism, then it should at least be given a new name (isn't that what marketing consultants persuade their manufacturers to do when a product has gone stale?).

If a definition is required for the whole range of new architecture that is starting to be produced, then perhaps 'humanism' is a good term – an architecture on the human scale, sympathetic to the user and viewer. The Henry Ford choice of, 'You can have any architecture you like as long as it is Modernist' is giving way to a more user-friendly architecture for the public. Society can now demand variety.

8 Modernism is Dead

Modernism has failed in its primary aim to improve the lives of ordinary people. It attempted to achieve too much too quickly. Mass-scale planning did away with traditional urban lifestyles and, street patterns. Mass production and standardization produced bland, often poorly constructed buildings. Technology was pushed beyond its limits, which led to major structural weaknesses. The new materials laid Modernism open to abuse by get-rich-quick developers and people's needs were left behind in the rush. At its best Modernism has worked spectacularly well – when small-scale and well built – but it simply does not work in any context in the hands of second-raters. While the man and woman in the street have long been questioning the merits of the new-style architecture, the design profession only really began to smart when Prince Charles launched his attack on contemporary building.

The shock of the new

Aesthetics are always a subjective matter, and Prince Charles stirred up considerable resentment among key Modernists such as Richard Rogers, James Stirling, Norman Foster and my successor at the RIBA, Maxwell Hutchinson by favouring traditional styles. He found little to praise in Modernism and so was lambasted for being backward-looking. Richard Rogers wrote in *The Times* on 3 July 1989:

If the conservative principles favoured by the Prince of Wales and his followers had been applied throughout history very little of our 'traditional' architectural heritage would ever have been built. Most of the great buildings in the Classical and Gothic traditions which the conservationists value so highly were, in their own time, revolutionary. If buildings like the great Gothic churches, the palazzi of Renaissance Italy or St Paul's seem to us to exist in a harmonious relation with their neighbours, it is not because they slavishly imitated them in size, style or material. Rather they embodied new building techniques and distinctive architectural forms quite unlike anything ever seen before.

Without taking issue with his basic argument, it is worthwhile remembering that the examples of revolutionary design that he gives all had key factors in their favour – they were well built, using quality materials and skilled labour.

In truth, the Prince of Wales and his critics share a considerable area of common ground. HRH, Maxwell Hutchinson and Richard Rogers, if only they knew it, are really on the same side. They each want better quality buildings and environments, and stand for the advancement of architecture.

Back to the future

Thrown by the critics, the architectural profession has suffered a loss of nerve, and the new fad is for producing historical pastiches. I have seen buildings which incorporate everything from Tudor beams to Classical arches in the same design. There are few things more ugly and reprehensible than neo-Georgian and Tudorbethan housing estates and neo-Classical, plastic Post-Modernist supermarkets and shopping complexes.

Nevertheless I am convinced that we cannot turn our backs on the past and ignore our inheritance. We owe a great debt to our ancestors. Why tamper with building styles and methods which have been proven to work? Why not produce homes which are solid, comfortable, secure and easy to maintain, which people can enjoy and be proud of? And towns and cities which are designed to a human scale and which are pleasant to work and shop in?

I have frequently been criticized for being old-fashioned and folksy, but I cannot accept that appreciation of good-quality workmanship and pleasing, effective design is a fault. Traditional stone- and brick-built houses are design classics; so too are the great Victorian industrial and municipal buildings. Even Modernist blocks of flats (when well built and well managed) can provide perfect accommodation for those people who like to live close to the centre of bustling city life.

Experiments in innovative design are least harmful when applied to prestige company buildings, or public buildings like art galleries, airports and railway stations. Fortunately a number of major companies, such as Sainsbury's and Lloyd's, have recognized their responsibilities to the environment and have taken care to encourage interesting, quality architecture. Rogers' statement, exemplified by his own work – the Pompidou Centre and the Lloyd's Building – prove that good Modernist architecture is more than just a pretty façade. And this is where the current debate is now concentrated.

Strategic planning, adequate investment (in both time and money), the use of thoroughly tested materials, trained labour, a caring approach and public consultation must be combined with skilful design to produce buildings which people can enjoy and the architectural profession can be proud of. Here, again, the Prince of Wales and his critics are united. As Maxwell Hutchinson said in his inaugural speech as president of the RIBA in the summer of 1989: 'We achieve nothing of worth if the perception of our achievement is worthless. We fail in our duty to society if (for its part) society does not encourage and insist on the very best from us.'

Never mind the width

The lack of adequate investment is largely to blame for so much poor work. For too long in Britain the cheap solution has been sought. We have lost sight of the fact that architecture is the most visible of all the arts. It you don't like Picasso's paintings you don't visit the exhibition, but you cannot avoid looking at buildings every day of your life. And architecture is not only constantly on show – it is also an integral part of the landscape or street scene.

Designers should therefore always remember that they have a responsibility to produce buildings of a sufficiently high quality – in exterior and interior design as well as in construction – to withstand the rigours of time and the demands of change. Here the Modern Movement has failed countless times. In the pursuit of quality, Mitterrand's Paris is a prime example to follow. Generous budgets and tough design competitions have produced some of the finest new buildings this century.

If we are to succeed in the future, a climate must be created in which good design can flourish through an emphasis on quality – from the planning stage through to design, construction and renovation, and in researching and understanding people's needs. No one element can be separated from the others.

The creed of greed

Much of what has been built during the past decade stands now as a symbol of the greediness of the eighties. It is the attitude of avaricious developers that has caused the most damage – they have not been keen to build ten charming homes with gardens and a carefully landscaped setting on a plot of land where it is possible to make more money from a concentration of fifty considerably smaller apartments. The London Docklands is a prime example.

During the eighties Britain witnessed a dramatic U-turn in urban planning. In complete contrast to the restrictive and formal zoning laws which designated separate areas for housing and commerce, London Docklands was declared an Enterprise Zone in which all planning constraint was waived. The result is an area with absolutely no coherence.

Relaxation of controls was a deliberate ploy to entice developers' money. They could build what they liked, where they liked. But because of the lack of design guidelines there is virtually no infrastructure – no adequate public amenities, not enough green spaces nor attractive vistas, and no proper roads and public transport systems.

However, the Docklands developers are now having to count the cost of their greed. No longer can they call the tune. Many of the new complexes are rapidly losing their appeal to potential buyers because homes are cramped, access difficult, there are no schools for their children and it is miles to the nearest shops – the same old problems of the municipal Modernist estates!

The jumble of styles will remain an eyesore. It was aptly described by the editor of the *Architect's Journal* as a vision which has 'lurched drunkenly from suburban business park, to pseudo Amsterdam, to miniature Manhattan and finally complete visual chaos'.

It may be too late to rescue vast tracts of the newly constructed Docklands, but there are hopeful signs of change in the latest stage of development at the Royal Docks. Already there is encouraging talk of master planning and drafting of design guidelines at the Royal Victoria Dock. The London Docklands Development Corporation, once proud of its *carte blanche*, do-as-you-please approach, has seen the error of its ways. A massive £175 million has been spent on infrastructure at the Royal Victoria Docks. Even before developers have begun to dig foundations, roads, pavements and public spaces are in place and at last local residents are being offered the chance to play their part in the consultation process.

The value of a well-conceived and sensibly executed infra-structure cannot be overstated. For too long the architectural debate has been narrowly focused on the question of style. The obsession with judging a building by its frontage – façadism – is, by definition, superficial.

Of course, the look of a structure has an immediate impact on the streetscape, but we should also look at its effect on a community – whether that building is required in the first place, whether it is the right size, whether it answers the needs of its occupants. Many more developers and architects are now seeing these considerations as fundamental to the process of obtaining planning permission from conscientious councils and finding buyers.

The eye of the storm

The question of tackling redevelopment has reached a crucial stage and is the focus of considerable press publicity. Now, at the eleventh hour, historic sites are at the centre of attention, particularly those in the City of London. The long-running row over Paternoster Square is now approaching a resolution. The City of London planners, in 1988, gave notice that they would refuse planning permission for developments unless designs treated the site, in the hands of several owners, as a whole. At the time of writing this idea appears to be possible through the formation of an alliance of the landowners.

On the south side of St Paul's the 1.8-acre Petershill site may well become the national testing ground for handling such sensitive areas. A great community architect, Ted Cullinan, has been awarded the commission as a result of a design competition. Although his designs have yet to be finalized, Cullinan won the competition to replace the nondescript sixties' commercial archi-tecture on the strength of his sensitive planning ideas. The assessors liked his work because it 'suggested the most human office spaces', and proposed 'external spaces which offered a great variety of interest to the public as well as office users'.

The brief from the site's leaseholders, MEPC, was for a substantial quantity of office building. However, in his initial plans Cullinan has succeeded in downplaying the enormous bulk of commercial space. He has avoided the temptation to build one massive block, and suggests the construction of a number of buildings of varying sizes. To ensure that the new work is in keeping with its surroundings he has proposed it should be built in traditional brick and Portland stone. His ideas recreate some of the old charm of the area and also include a reconstruction of Wren's tower to St Mary Magdalen Church, which stood on the site until the 1880s, the provision of a central leafy courtyard space, and the opening up of vistas to St Paul's and various City churches.

Model approaches

Prince Charles has adopted a model approach to urban planning with his own housing scheme on land that he owns in Dorchester, Dorset. Having selected the RIBA Gold Medallist Leon Krier as architect-cum-master planner, the Prince has once again raised the temperature of debate on style – Krier plans to build a completely traditional village, or, to be more accurate, a series of villages covering an area of some 450 acres – and has also brought the question of planning to the forefront.

Krier is a great believer in creating areas in which uses are integrated – where shops, offices, houses, schools, theatres, cinemas, restaurants and light industry are all within easy reach on foot. Like me, he believes that when the scale is controlled people usually feel less threatened. The mixture of uses means the streets do not revert to forbidding wastelands once the shops and offices close, and people have the opportunity to live close to their work and so don't need to jam the roads with their cars.

Krier also shares my feeling that the most successful cities result from sensitive planning, and holds Haussmann's nineteenth-century Paris – a city composed of quarters, each built on a human scale – as an ideal model of urban design. Baltimore, too, is a shining example of thorough planning and preparation; it was built to a master plan with design guidelines. From a sprawling, dangerous and unattractive backwater, one of the most ambitious of America's waterside redevelopments has transformed it into a thriving and far safer city.

The Prince has encouraged the local Dorchester community to take part in the planning process and has held a series of seminars to determine the most pressing needs of the population. When the people complained that they felt the development was too big, the response was to scale it down.

A chorus of disapproval

The willingness of the public to take a stand has also been demonstrated in Birmingham, where plans are underway to redesign the city centre. Here the strength of feeling and concern has resulted in the formation of a group called Birmingham For People. Not only has it spoken out strongly against proposals by its owner, the London and Edinburgh Trust, but it has drawn up its own suggestions. The most hotly contested site is the Bull Ring.

Architects Chapman Taylor Partners' design was for a replacement scheme called The Galleries – a solid block of one million square feet of shopping behind a curved neo-Classical façade. But, as Birmingham For People quickly pointed out, the council's lack of urban design policy allowed developers to offer a scheme with limited pedestrian access, wide roads, no attractive vistas, parking for around 3500 cars and complete freedom over the scale of buildings. The People's Plan is very different – it would involve the phased construction of small-scale buildings, a metro line delivering shoppers right to the heart of the development, a large outdoor market area, plenty of public spaces and limited access for cars.

At the time of going to press the developers have chosen to ignore the People's Plan and have made no moves to set up a forum for public consultation. Chapman Taylor's own plans have yet to be approved by the city council. Says Joe Holyoak of the People's group:

> Birmingham For People is urging the city council to accept its strategies as council policy for the Bull Ring. It is a traditional plan, which in the context of modern Birmingham makes it very radical indeed. It has the successful traditional qualities which are found in Birmingham's sister cities of Milan, Frankfurt and Barcelona, the category of which Birmingham so much aspires to join as a great European city.
>
> If Birmingham City Council approves the detailed planning application for The Galleries it will not only be shooting itself in the foot, as it has done so many times before; it will be blowing off its entire leg. For the sake of its people's quality of life, and its national and international reputation, Birmingham must listen to its citizens and get it right this time.

Inviting people for their comments is, I believe, fundamental to the production of good architecture. It was certainly an element noticeably lacking during the reign of the Modernists. When people are consulted and kept informed, they are far more likely to take an interest in their environment and far less likely to accept the word of professionals who claim to know what is best.

Heritage trail

One of the most encouraging of recent trends is the increase in

174

refurbishment of older property: interesting and sympathetic conversions of old buildings into flats have proved highly marketable. In tackling these tasks we can learn a great deal from America, where in every state the care taken to preserve character is exemplary. The 'greening' of the British consciousness is sure to bring pressure to bear on developments here.

Much building in Britain, particularly during the late eighties' boom in business parks, shopping complexes and housing, has been concentrated on the edges of towns and cities, draining the centres of their life-blood. However, a similar flow has been stemmed in America where tax incentives, introduced by the government to play a key role in urban regeneration, allow the developer to write off acquisition and conversion costs. The unscrupulous are kept in check with strict federal guidelines which penalize unsympathetic work – particularly in renovation projects. Where a scheme is considered too radical, the developer stands to lose the tax benefits. It has proved to be an effective deterrent.

These guidelines are far-reaching and demand that the developers contribute more than merely saving fascias; they are also required to preserve original material, architectural features and hardware wherever possible – for example stairs, elevators, handrails, balusters, cornices, skirtings, doorways, windows, light fixtures, parquet or mosaic flooring and even wallpapers and paints.

Constructing contemporary extensions is not forbidden, but again the guidelines insist that any new building is sympathetic to the surroundings. Architects are expected to respect existing styles, materials, colours and scale.

Incriminating evidence

This American approach – promoting the use of local materials and styles – makes perfect sense to me, to Prince Charles and a large proportion of the general public, and yet a survey in the *Architects' Journal* published in September 1989 demonstrated just how differently the majority of professionals feel.

The survey offered a fascinating insight into the disparities which exist between the profession and its most outspoken critic, the Prince of Wales.

While 78 per cent agreed that the Prince should continue to speak out about architecture (interestingly, the figure was 87 per cent for young architects under 35), 66 per cent disagreed strongly with the Prince's proposal that Classical styles were intrinsically better than Modern.

When architects were asked whether they agreed with the Prince that local traditional styles produced better architecture than modern styles 35 per cent said they did agree, but 65 per cent said they did not. They were only a little more enthusiastic about the use of traditional building materials – 41 per cent were in favour, but 59 per cent against.

With this disheartening evidence of how the profession still thinks, it is clear that the public will have to continue to play an active role in building projects, either by making their protests clearly heard, or by building for themselves or with the help of a community architecture practice.

At least one encouraging figure to emerge from the *Architects' Journal* survey related to the Prince's advocacy of community architecture – 65 per cent of architects polled approved of the Prince's stand. Most encouraging of all was the change in thinking indicated among younger designers – of architects under 40, 74 per cent approved.

Community architecture in practice

My architectural practice is not typical by any means, but, although the workload has increased, it still operates on the same basic principles I learned when I first started out twenty years ago at Black Road. I began as a community architect and have never lost my initial enthusiasm for helping people beat the system and take control of their own homes. But I have also branched out into other areas – primarily refurbishment of old properties and building good-quality new housing – so that my current spread of work is around 25 per cent community architecture, 35 per cent refurbishment and 40 per cent new construction. Preserving the best from the past and building the new which has an immediate sense of place form the basis of my own way of working.

The architects I employ must, of necessity, have a rare mix of qualities; it is essential that they are good at handling people, as well as being able to explain projects in a clear, straightforward way. They have also to be adept diplomats and able to cope with the considerable amount of negotiating that always has to be undertaken with local councils, which leaves no room for prima donnas.

Each project has a site office where the architect in charge is on call around the clock. Whatever the scheme, it is essential to build and maintain close contacts with local people, so that any barriers are broken down and everyone can be kept abreast of progress.

I often think of us as being rather like missionaries – going into an area to solve problems, boosting the confidence of the people we are working with, and passing on skills. Breathing new life into an area is not achieved by simply refurbishing or building – it runs much deeper than that, encompassing everything from teaching practical skills to encouraging people to stand up for themselves and instilling a sense of pride in their environment.

Successful and lasting regeneration does not come from a neat package of instructions. Each project has its own idiosyncrasies, and so the architects involved must be enormously versatile. They must be able to turn their hand to a vast repertoire of jobs – from chairing meetings and organizing grants to sorting out plumbing or electrical wiring problems. This spread of knowledge ensures continuity – people involved in the schemes know who they can turn to for help – which dispels the intimidating cloak of professional mystique. Many practices employ several architects for each job – a designer, a contracts architect and a supervisor – but our schemes employ one leader who co-ordinates the rest of the team and sees the job through from start to finish.

To ensure the best possible quality of work we also employ our own builders. Some are craftsmen who have been employed for a number of years, while the rest are people who have learned their skills from our self-help schemes. That way we are able to give men and women, many of whom were formerly unemployed, a stronger chance in the job market.

Work on each project begins life in the Macclesfield head-quarters where my own involvement starts with finding the right architect to lead the team, taking part in initial negotiations with local councils, meeting residents and securing funding. Once work has started, regular site visits keep me in constant touch with progress.

Roan Court – new homes for old

My own ideas for building a good housing estate were put into practice in a development in Macclesfield. Roan Court is new – but it is the complete antithesis of the majority of new estates springing up around the country. A three-acre canalside plot of once-derelict land is now an estate of sixty homes built in a traditional, vernacular style – a project for which I acted as developer, planner, designer and builder.

Varying in size from around 1000 to 1500 square feet, the homes were designed for a mix of residents from young single people to families. Unlike most community schemes, which involve renovation, the homes here were built from scratch, but many buyers were involved from the start to ensure the finished product suited their needs.

To avoid the blandness and hard, new look of so many

developments Roan Court was specially constructed to blend into its surroundings. Where many builders might have been tempted to bulldoze the site to one level, we kept the contours of the land as a feature. And where others would have used new materials we used recycled ones – oak timbers from demolished barns, bricks from mills, flagstones from sites in Manchester, cobbles from Liverpool, blue tiles from Stoke-on-Trent, stone slates from Kerridge and even weathervanes and clock faces from dismantled clock towers. Where old materials were not available they were reproduced – for example, plastic rainwater guttering was rejected in favour of traditional wooden gutters which were made from 6x4 inch timbers.

Recycled materials are more expensive than their mass-produced modern counterparts, but they last longer and certainly look more appealing. Construction, at around nine months per home, is also more time-consuming than, say, an average Wimpey home, but the results speak for themselves. Each property was sold either while it was still on the drawing board or before work was completed on site.

The Burnley triangle – homes that work

One of my most interesting and challenging renovation projects was carried out in Burnley in Lancashire. In the mid-eighties I was invited by Burnley Borough Council to prepare a report on how to save the town's Weavers' Triangle – a complex of disused Victorian cotton mills.

The buildings had great charm. Like Roan Court they were sited alongside a canal and were of superb quality – built when the Lancashire mill towns were thriving and people talked about 'King Cotton'. The mills had been spared demolition during the sixties and seventies simply because the area was too poor to attract developers.

I discovered that there were many local people running small businesses who wanted to live close to their work, and so we proposed turning the old industrial buildings into homes with workshops attached. The idea of working and living on the same premises is, of course, nothing new and operates on exactly the same principle as the pre-industrial weavers' cottages that are still found dotted around the area.

Along with developers Lancashire Enterprise, my practice bought up some of the property. Work began on one section, known as Bank Parade. Our scheme, called Stackhouses, is the pilot. It consists of a blend of housing and 1000 square foot workshops adjoining apartments of the same size.

The idea of mixing uses caused a few raised eyebrows in the council chamber. At first the local authority, still obsessed with Modernist ideas of zoning, was reluctant to grant planning permission for the project because it proposed residential development next to industrial. However, our perseverance paid off, and once the authority saw how much interest was generated, it became a great ally of the scheme.

Rescue operation

In the light of all that has been learned during the past few decades it seems incredible that there are councils still threatening to demolish vast areas of homes. Yet, in the late eighties, the Labour-controlled Stoke City Council was laying plans to flatten around 20 acres – some three thousand terrace houses – in the old pottery town of Tunstall. And this over twenty years after central government introduced the 1969 Housing Act to encourage refurbishment in place of destruction!

The residents of Hawes Street contacted my practice for help early in 1987. I had always had an affinity with Stoke-on-Trent, as it was my mother's birthplace – we used to spend Christmas there with my grandmother in her three-up-three-down terrace house, and so I have a strong affection for the place and its people. When I arrived in Tunstall I was shocked to see how much demolition had already been carried out. The town was poor and had suffered since the collapse of the pottery industry, but the remaining housing, although run down, was perfectly sound. It consisted of rows of typical Victorian Potteries homes, brick-faced with blue-tiled roofs and sash windows, just as I remembered from my childhood. As soon as I began talking to the local people I knew they had the special qualities of courage and determination which could save their homes.

Their story unfolded. In the autumn of 1984 the city council had designated the area for 'community renewal' – a curious euphemism for demolition. No one had been told they would lose their homes, and the fact was only discovered by chance during a local search when one householder tried to sell his property. It was a heartless council decision which demonstrated a complete indifference to the fate of Tunstall people.

From then on it was a familiar pattern of events. The council bought up large numbers of homes from people wanting to leave the area, then boarded them up and left them to rot – so encouraging vandals. Despite the council's stated intention to demolish, the place had just been left in limbo. It wasn't long before concern reached such a pitch among the remaining occupants that the local Labour Party decided to hold a meeting and allow residents to protest publicly.

In the autumn of 1986, in a tremendous show of strength, over two hundred local people turned up at a meeting to state their case to the various councillors, including the leader, Ron Southern. The members sat bravely while they listened to endless condemnations of their insensitive attitude towards residents – before eventually admitting that their demolition programme was already threatened because of lack of financial support from central government (it had been many years since government supported slum clearance programmes).

However, the council made no promise to curtail its plans, and so the next day a group of residents formed the Hawes Street Residents' Association. Under the leadership of kiln operator Keith Dawkins the community, now closer than it had ever been, decided to refuse offers of high-rise council flats and set out to save its homes.

The Hawes Street people were admirably resilient and inventive. One shop owner, Eddie Steele, used his outside walls to display enormous posters emblazoned with the message; 'Welcome to another Compulsory Purchase Order area'. He had lost a considerable amount of trade through the council plans and, knowing he would not be included in any council-led regeneration programme, demanded fair compensation. He wanted £40,000, but was offered only £9500 for his life's endeavours. He even took his case to the European Court of Human Rights – but lost. Eventually, when he refused to move, he was arrested. Shortly after, the bulldozers reduced his shop to a pile of rubble. Eddie Steele was just one victim of the demolition process. There have been many other shattered lives caused unnecessarily by the council's outmoded belief in slum clearance.

Then the city council heard that its allocation from central government was being cut yet further. It was a godsend for local people and forced the authority to rethink its housing policy. Letters were sent to lobby local councillors for support.

The media was called on for help, too. A lucky twist of fate saw the Tunstall situation come to a head at the same time as I became president of the RIBA, in the summer of 1987. My work was to be featured in an *Omnibus* television programme, and I was able to include the Tunstall story. Cameras were invited into one of the major Hawes Street residents' meetings, where June Daniels from Black Road and I explained how community schemes worked.

June was a star. She told everyone at the meeting that it had taken 1700 hours of hard work to rebuild her home. It had been no easy task, but the results had been well worthwhile. 'I cried more than I laughed, but now I am so proud of what we have done in Macclesfield,' she said.

182

Meanwhile Stoke City Council was still refusing to change its mind about demolition and was continuing with its campaign to squeeze more money from central government. In a report the council declared that more than half the city's housing was unfit for human habitation; 54,000 of its 92,000 homes were in urgent need of repairs and some £163 million was needed to bring the 30,000 council homes up to scratch. It was claimed that no other city in the United Kingdom faced such appalling problems. The council was hoping to use the figures to prise more money from central government – but the scheme backfired because for some people in central government it must have seemed that the picture only demonstrated further Stoke's ineptitude at managing housing.

It was a frustrating time. There were clearly insufficient funds in the kitty to repair housing overnight, but the council still seemed unwilling to recognize that there was a sizeable body of people in Stoke ready and willing to help themselves. By this time, too, over ten thousand successful General Improvement Area schemes had been completed in Britain – the council had no reason to continue ignoring our pleas.

There were a few glimmers of hope – local support continued to snowball, letters appeared in the papers, the council opened up some of its disused properties to take people from the growing waiting lists, and with sponsorship from local firms some of the people created a community garden. It was the first symbol of people working together to improve their run-down area.

The Reverend David Watkin took over the chairmanship of the Hawes Street residents' association. He was a trained accountant and was able to give the association much-needed financial help as well as being a political leader.

I then set up an office in the area to provide a base for my team of assistants, where we set to work drawing detailed plans and costings for the Hawes Street refurbishment. We also prepared a report to submit to the council's Housing and Health Committee in the spring of 1988, hoping that they would adopt our proposals for regeneration in place of demolition.

Our findings showed that the properties in Hawes Street and the surrounding area were in substantially good condition and would cost less than £20,000 each to improve, guaranteeing a further life of at least thirty years. The council would have faced an average cost of £32,000 for each new home built, plus a minimum of £10,000 compensation to each householder. Our redevelopment plans would have cost £3–5 million to complete, compared with the council's sum of around £14 million for demolition and redevelopment. The figures spoke for themselves.

Outside support was then offered. Local companies such as Ibstock Bricks and Twyfords offered building materials and house fittings, while the Church Urban Fund offered money, as did Inner City Aid, the Civic Trust and Telethon. The Neighbourhood Revitalization Scheme chipped in with offers of free professional advice. Yet still the council doubted residents' commitment and showed no signs of adopting our proposals.

Then Stoke City Council came under severe attack from the then Housing Minister, William Waldegrave. In an interview with Stoke's *Evening Sentinel* he criticized the council for failing to use up its Housing Improvement Programme allocation:

> It is not an exaggeration to say that Stoke does not spring to mind as leading the way with housing solution problems. My advice to Stoke is that it should be realistic. It must develop a coherent housing strategy. It must have a proper plan to put to us to deal with the problems. If Stoke-on-Trent gets its act together in a sensible way then we will respond.
>
> I am looking forward to a new regime in Stoke and then we may be able to direct more resources there. If they put their thinking caps on and come halfway to meet us, then we are prepared to respond positively.

It was a clear directive from the minister to Stoke Council that they should start talking to local people. Shortly afterwards, the *Sentinel* published some disturbing figures produced by the

Department of the Environment. As William Waldegrave had said, the council had failed to use all its housing improvement money: the amount unspent between 1978 and 1982 was a staggering £4.3 million. It was also revealed at this time that the city council had plans to build just twenty-one houses in 1988.

A flurry of council activity followed: Stanley Street in Tunstall was declared a General Improvement Area; a £120,000 facelift programme for tenants' gardens in Fenton was announced; and plans were put forward to reclaim over 600 acres of derelict land. Top of the list was Tunstall. In addition the CBI proposed a major private sector initiative to pump millions of pounds into Stoke – by both creating jobs and building new homes and factories. Bond Street was declared Tunstall's second General Improvement Area, and then an £8 million facelift was announced for Shelton – Stoke's largest urban regeneration programme, taking in some two thousand houses.

But there was still no news for the Hawes Street residents. They had to wait until 7 November 1988 before a report appeared in the *Sentinel*, declaring that the council had decided to give the go-ahead to the do-it-yourself scheme. The official GIA announcement was not made until 16 December, more than four years after the campaign to save the homes had begun.

Plans have been drawn up and work has now started on a core of 350 homes. The tenants have formed a building and development co-operative and have agreed to buy the 106 council-owned properties in the area. Mortgages have been secured with the Halifax Building Society. Further financial help was also sought in improvement grants. The majority of residents are undertaking the building work themselves – and not just to the inside of homes, but also to pavements, steps, gates, street lamps and walls. All the work is being carried out in close association with the council.

Residents are fully aware of the hard slog they have ahead of them, but already their story has been turned into a musical, *Good Golly Miss Molly*, by Bob Eaton, which showed to packed houses at Stoke's Victoria Theatre. The cast couldn't fail to become enthused and took part in a benefit performance to raise money for the Hawes Street residents. As the *Guardian*'s critic, Robin Thornber, said: 'This is the best of the current vogue for rock musicals because it has something to say that's worth hearing. There's something satisfying about a celebration of such community spirit.'

9 Hackney's Empire

As a nation we have a rich history of design and craftmanship. Building, masonry and engineering expertise, beautiful woodwork, metalwork, paintings, furniture, ceramics, glass and fabrics are a heritage that we almost take for granted. But these achievements, created over the centuries, are a far cry from the cheap, mass-produced debris found everywhere today. So where did we go wrong?

Quality work was done by highly skilled craftsmen and women who learned their trades as apprentices to masters. The commissions came from wealthy patrons. The industrial revolution opened the doors to mass production. The possibility of producing more for less became so attractive that quality was sacrificed for quantity. Consumers grew accustomed to buying inferior products. However, now the pendulum is swinging back.

The food industry illustrates perhaps most clearly how, literally, tastes have changed. Many people now choose to buy real ale instead of mass-produced bitter. They prefer traditionally baked bread from small bakeries to the factory-produced white sliced loaf, and fresh farm eggs to those from battery hens.

A similar trend away from blandness and mass production is also happening in design. Products will undoubtedly cost more, but, as clearly illustrated by the cheap buildings of the sixties, a larger outlay in the first place would have saved a great deal of expense in the long run.

Ways of seeing

As with food, people need re-educating to be able to tell the difference between good and bad, and that can start at school. The creation of a well-built future relies, as with most structures, on laying sound foundations. In Britain, before we can hope to make any great strides in improving our environment we have an urgent need to improve the nature of education. Few British schools pay any attention to the subject of design. The system operates in such a way that art is treated as a 'soft' subject inferior to any academic study.

No two people will share exactly the same tastes, but even a simple exercise in colour co-ordination will help raise awareness of which shades look well together and which don't. Good-quality design can also be measured using the most elementary yard-stick: does the product fulfil the function for which it was made, and has it been sufficiently well produced to last? A radical change in approach must be made so that design appears on every curriculum. Only then will youngsters be encouraged to look more critically and develop into a visually literate adult population which can influence the environment for the benefit of everyone.

The master builder

I firmly believe, as Arne Jacobsen did, in the concept of the architect as the universal man or woman. The ideal architect should combine a number of skills such as engineering, design and building, but above all should possess vision and the ability to make the most of a difficult site, a complicated brief and perhaps limited funding. The architect should be seen as a project co-ordinator – someone who understands the requirements of both client and user, and is then able to draw upon the skills of engineers, planners, surveyors and builders to fulfil the brief.

In order to achieve this an altogether more practical approach has to be nurtured in training. Most tutors, although trained architects, spend their working lives teaching, but how much more valuable it would be to have more practising architects invited to lecture. There is no better way for students to keep abreast of current problems and advances than by finding out from someone who is working in the field.

My own architectural education was woefully lacking in two main areas – an appreciation of small-scale projects, and practical knowledge of traditional building skills and materials. These I have learned the hard way, through experience. There is no reason why architects today should not be taught basic skills such as bricklaying or joinery. This is invaluable to the understanding of the practical transition from drawing board to completed building.

This change of academic emphasis would also help to break down the unnecessary barriers between architect and builder and so bring the two closer together. In Britain, particularly, there currently exists a clear and obstructive distinction between manual workers and professionals in the building business. If the two understood each other's work more thoroughly, as indeed they do in Italy and Spain, we would see more mutual respect and a harmonized approach to building.

The existing divide costs time and money. A large proportion of class time at architecture school is spent on explaining how to cope with legal cases involving designers, clients and builders. A better understanding and thorough consultation at the start of a project could easily prevent building mistakes, which in turn would increase production and pre-empt costly and time-consuming litigation.

Tunnel vision

Architecture schools are also responsible for fostering a lack of vision. Designs are not always made, nor materials selected, with the future in mind.

Many tutors adopt a narrow approach to large projects and treat a major new building as a piece of sculpture unrelated to its surroundings. The results of this attitude lead to some of the public's bitterest complaints that new buildings simply don't 'fit in'. Architects should always take care to ensure that continuity is maintained in the area immediately surrounding the new work. It can be achieved through scale, materials, styles – or all three. With this in mind, it is still possible to experiment and be innovative.

Denys Lasdun, for example, achieved a huge success with his uncompromisingly Modernist building for the Royal College of Physicians. In the highly sensitive area of London's Regent's Park, surrounded by the beautiful John Nash terraces, it could so easily have been disastrous. Despite the fact that it is a simple block, built on columns and finished in white ceramic tiles, the careful use of scale and understatement makes it a handsome building.

Art schools also continue to fall into the trap of promoting the use of new and often untested materials. Naturally enough, students are eager to make advances and will not be satisfied with constantly looking to the past. However, although many manufacturers of new construction materials invest considerable energy into the promotion of their products, this enthusiasm is rarely matched by research into their performance. The countless building disasters of the past few decades clearly demonstrate that it is essential to gather as much information as possible about new materials before they are widely used. Sadly, research is not given the attention it deserves, but if students are taught to ask more intelligent and searching questions about a material's performance then manufacturers will be pressed to provide the answers.

For too long many buildings have been constructed with little thought of their longevity. The throwaway culture of the sixties percolated into architecture. I would like to see schools impress on students the idea that a structure should be built to last, and should be appropriate in style and flexibility to cater for possible changes fifty or even a hundred years ahead.

Vox popular

Designing with the user in mind is of course another basic consideration. Changes are already perceptible. Where once people were considered a hindrance to good design their opinions are now being included as a part of the design process. We have all seen what happens when the public is alienated by poorly designed homes or shopping centres – they dislike them sufficiently to abuse or even destroy them. No one is going to damage or tear down a house they enjoy living in. Answering the needs of users is of equal importance to producing an innovative design. It is a strong alliance and the two should not be separated.

The RIBA was the first institution in the United Kingdom to bring in lay assessors to judge its design awards, and schools of architecture could easily follow suit. People from the business world could be invited to comment on new workshop and factory designs, housing association staff and residents could be asked for their views of house designs, nurses and even patients for opinions of hospital plans – and so on. A brief question-and-answer session between student and potential user would allow the student to explain how his or her project was intended to work. Once students have learned to account for their designs they are more likely to take users into account when they enter practice. This change of approach would provide a major encouragement to architects to think out their schemes carefully.

I would take the point even further and suggest that any schemes submitted to local councils for planning permission should first undergo public appraisal. Residents' groups currently make representations on new building projects to local authorities – but these are usually in the form of protests. However, if those same groups were invited to make critical appraisals and suggestions for improvement then a healthy exchange could be set up between developer, council and local people.

Educational changes are a long-term but no less necessary

objective. It may well be that beneficial effects will take at least two generations to have any impact. In the meantime there are many more immediate points.

The regeneration game

Numerous solutions to environmental problems, such as development corporations and enterprise zones, have been tried and failed. They are too narrowly focused – usually intent on job creation – and have not succeeded in broad-based regeneration which should stimulate long-term employment, improve housing and upgrade the entire environment. What is needed is a new, holistic approach.

Firstly, a centralized funding agency would be the most effective way to administer all the current government cash for inner cities. It should pay special attention to encouraging people to apply for repair and renovation grants, it should make the system easier, and it should help to sponsor professional advisers to community groups. The recent Housing Corporation boost of £40 million for self-help groups provides a typical example of poor government management – the money is offered, but to reach it people first have to work their way through a complicated mesh of bureaucracy and form-filling.

The funding agency could also encourage private investors, banks and building societies wholly or partly to finance regeneration schemes. The prospect would seem much more appealing if tax advantages were offered.

Secondly, government must realize that regeneration begins with homes and not jobs. It should therefore adopt a policy of treating people as a resource by encouraging more council tenants who are willing and able to restore their own homes.

The Department of Health and Social Security could assist by continuing to expand its programme for dole claimants who make a gradual transition into full-time employment. With the knowledge that they will have some income, unemployed people will be more likely to join self-help housing schemes where they can learn skills and earn some money as trainees.

It makes sound economic sense to encourage people to train. A typical family with unemployed parents could be costing the state in excess of £150 per week in family supplements, housing benefits and dole money. Once adults become skilled and find work, or set up on their own, they can easily be earning twice that, contributing to the national economy and returning money to the state in taxes.

Thirdly, we need a reappraisal of the planning laws. Zoning controls should be loosened, so that in neighbourhoods which are currently segregated they could be relaxed to allow a mix of homes, schools, offices, shops and some light industry.

Legislation must be made more locally applicable. At present the same book of rules governs towns, cities and rural areas. Planning offices could play a useful role in promoting the use of local materials in new developments.

Fourthly, architects should endeavour to forge closer links with community groups, an aim which could be achieved by setting up street corner offices. Where areas are undergoing renovation a small group of advisers could be given a local base and operate a design 'surgery'. The office staff could also include planners, engineers and builders, who would be paid either by contributions from the central agency, mentioned above, or through grants and other monies collected for each particular regeneration project in the area.

A model city

Let me take the example of an imaginary city to illustrate what I consider the best approach to problems which are common to many. If Le Corbusier could see how differently real cities have turned out compared with *his* model city, no doubt he would turn in his grave. However, the solutions do not depend on the expert and the machine, but rather on the residents themselves. My city is typical of a large number in Britain. Its centre consists of modern shopping precincts, a few remaining traditional shopping streets, office blocks, multi-storey car parks and disused industrial buildings. The centre is surrounded by an area of private housing, streets of derelict or dilapidated homes and half a dozen run-down council estates, followed by an outer ring of suburbs, a large industrial belt and several new out-of-town shopping complexes.

The majority of the problems facing the city are at the centre – in the council estates. Here crime and unemployment rates are high and the city authority is facing enormous bills in trying to maintain the buildings and surrounding wasteland.

In order to tackle the worst problems first in my imaginary city, let's look at typical Modernist housing estates close to the city centre. But first let's examine the background to the situation.

Many council blocks, as identified in the latest Housing Action Trusts survey undertaken by the DoE, have very little value as they stand. Individual flats can cost as much as £40,000 to renovate to a reasonable standard. Indeed the nationwide bill to repair our state housing is estimated in 1989 to be close to £200 billion. The chances of finding an immediate solution are slight – especially at a time when the entire housing budget is just £5 billion per annum – only 20 per cent of which is spent in inner cities.

The current Conservative government has pursued an enthusiastic policy of selling off council housing, and yet local authorities still manage 4.5 million housing units. Even more of these could usefully be sold off to their present occupiers. None the less, I also consider government has a moral obligation to continue providing homes to those people who prefer to rent, and more particularly to those who are elderly, ill or below the poverty line. Public money must be used to ensure that housing stocks continue to be made available and that they are maintained to far higher standards than at present.

Private investors have been encouraged to take over ownership of some well-kept council blocks, many of which have been converted into bijou apartments by large construction companies such as Regalian, Barratt and Wimpey. It is highly unlikely that these companies will adopt a philanthropic attitude towards the most needy, take on the refurbishment of crumbling blocks and provide low-cost housing. Indeed there are already signs that private investors are reluctant to tackle regeneration even of good-quality blocks of flats because of the high costs involved.

A number of councils, surprised at the response from investors, have called in experts to survey their stocks. To their dismay they have discovered that, far from being financial assets, many towers are liabilities and have no value. The bad news has been compounded by refusals from banks and building societies to give loans to potential buyers. Several towers have already been sold off, for as little as £1000, to developers for refurbishment, and within the next couple of years local authorities may well be faced with the prospect of either demolishing the blocks or paying people to take control of them.

The situation is grave. Councils have no money for repair work, private investors are not interested, housing associations are keeping a low profile. It would appear to make perfect sense to allow the residents themselves to take control. Unless this happens the deterioration can only accelerate, which will lead to the inevitable violent social response.

The renovation of any council estate should be considered a new industry for the area. Once the local people make a pledge to take control of their environment it immediately receives a tremendous boost. During the course of work, builders' merchants and hardware shops will open up nearby, along with a couple of building societies, grocery shops, small workshops, garages, light industry and so on, providing employment and an influx of money into the neighbourhood.

And yet ordinary people are being actively discouraged from becoming involved. It is a dangerous thing to underestimate human potential and the energy which can be generated when people are given the opportunity to help themselves. For too long council tenants have been regarded both as passive recipients of handouts and as the cause of problemms. They are not – they are actually the solution.

Local councils could easily take the initiative by starting a pilot project. Authorities must be aware that, because of the degree of mistrust which has grown up between officials and tenants, the approach should be handled with great care from the outset. Barriers must be broken down. The first move is to identify one estate and talk to residents to discover whether there is any potential for a self-help scheme. This can either be run with the entire block forming a co-operative ownership and management company, or by each tenant becoming an owner of his or her flat and the setting up of a tenants' association.

If there is no interest from residents, then the authority must decide either to continue as landlord or perhaps to encourage a housing association to take over the management. Empty or underused blocks which are hard to let could even be sold, or given, to colleges and universities as student accommodation. Or they could be converted into small workshops or schools – the possibilities are endless. Demolition is only a last resort.

Grant help

Incentives must form a part of the bargain. Individuals must be told that if they agree to enter a contract to restore their homes they will then be able to buy them for a nominal sum of perhaps £1000. The existing fitted bathrooms and kitchens are sure to be worth more than that alone, but prices are dictated by the quality and desirability of the area, which may be nil. It must also be agreed that the work is tackled as a whole and through team effort. There is no point in allowing half a dozen people in a block to become owners while others remain tenants. A reasonable time limit for the completion of work is also a useful discipline.

Local councils can offer help. They could either underwrite the financial risks, or offer to make available technical experts such as architects, planners, legal advisers and/or engineers.

And here the central government adoption of a scheme such as NURA, recommended by the RIBA's Inner Cities Committee, could provide further assistance. Grants for basic works such as reinforcing structures, and improving plumbing and fixtures in kitchens and bathrooms, should be made easily accessible.

The grants system is currently so knotted in bureaucracy that even experts find it difficult to unravel the red tape. Forms are intimidating and the rules are unnecessarily complicated. There can be so many frustrating stipulations. I remember one Black Road resident who needed a grant for a new door and frame, but was told that to qualify she would have to knock down a section of one wall and expand the size of the opening from a height of around 5ft 10ins to 6ft 6ins. She declined and bought her own door – the building work would have cost more than the grant money and, besides, since she stood at only 4ft 8ins she couldn't see the reason for installing a 6ft 6ins doorway. In another project I was remodelling small bathrooms. There was just enough room for a 5ft bath but I was told that a grant would only be available if I installed baths of 5ft 6ins. The regulation length was considered to hold sufficient water to clean oneself, whereas the shorter bath failed to comply. In fact, the 5ft bath held more water because of its steep sides!

In addition to grants, money for the works must also be found through building societies and banks. These financial institutions have already shown tremendous promise and foresight. Many, such as the Abbey National and Scottish Building Society at one of my projects in Stirling, Scotland, have taken the step of recognizing dole payments as regular income and have made loans on that basis.

Further advances are also possible. If a residents' group makes an approach as a renovation company, like any other commercial venture, their request should be considered on its potential. After all, building societies and banks can reap enormous profits in helping to secure the upward mobility of an area – if the worst buildings are improved, then the entire neighbourhood improves and property prices will naturally rise.

Comparatively small loans are already made to people who have shown initiative, learned skills and demonstrated that they can be self-supporting. Clearly, once they have joined the home-ownership ladder they will become valuable customers. Perhaps we will also soon see, as in Scandinavian countries, mortgages spread over longer periods than the traditional twenty to twenty-five years. Young people applying for loans before they are thirty could perhaps be offered a thirty-year repayment time; alternatively the repayments could be stretched to fifty years and passed from parents to their children.

Hesitancy on the part of banks and building societies often makes it difficult to secure a complete loan for one project. In those cases the finance can be found in stages. One lump sum could be paid at the beginning to set work in motion, and then as the scheme progresses, and the area improves in value, it should become possible to borrow more against the partially restored buildings.

During the late eighties loan repayments are becoming prohibitive because of increased interest rates – but now, more than ever, it is important to see funds injected into poor areas. The government could step in here once again and offer cut-price loans to those involved in inner city schemes. There are some encouraging moves in the right direction, but on nothing like a large enough scale.

Project monies can be found through the numerous government grants. These are available, for example, via the Urban Programme (annual budget of around £300 million) which sponsors joint enterprises run by local authorities and companies or voluntary groups; via City Grants (annual budget of around £17.5 million), paid to business investors prepared to develop inner city sites; via Derelict Land Grants (£81 million annual budget), paid to assist reclamation of disused industrial land; via the Urban Development Corporation (£124 million budget), for the physical, social and economic regeneration of designated areas; via Task Forces (£16 million annual budget) of civil servants working in areas of high need to promote small-scale enterprise and environmental improvement; and via Estate Action (£190 million annual budget), designed to improve council housing. In addition to these funds a range of Home Improvement Grants is available from local authorities for basic facilities such as bathrooms and toilets; for urgent structural work to strengthen walls, roofs, floors and foundations; for urgent rewiring and plumbing, insulation, damp-proofing and so on.

Cheap at half the price

To illustrate how funding can work let's take the example of an area of a hundred inner city flats built in the sixties. The land has no inherent value and the poor-condition buildings are worth a nominal sum of £1000 each for the freehold. Each flat requires around £40,000 to be spent on repairs and so the problem looks enormous – a total cost of over £4 million. However, if residents take charge I would estimate an immediate saving of around £10,000 per unit through the adoption of a small-scale approach with a devolution of control and limited bureaucracy. A further £10,000 could be saved if residents carried out the bulk of their own repairs – thereby halving the costs of the entire scheme.

A mortgage of just £21,000 would then be required by each householder – £20,000 for materials, an architect and administration, plus £1000 for acquisition. Repayments on this loan would be less than current council rents.

The final results would be an improvement to an overall equity value in excess of £4 million. The cost of this improvement would be just £2 million.

Outside in

The work of renovation should start with outside areas. This demonstrates to the neighbourhood that changes are on the way; in addition, fences and gates deter intruders and help residents visibly stake their claim on the property. The vacant open grassland and disused car parks around the base of blocks should either be fenced off and used by people living in the ground floor flats, turned into allotments, or, if there is a great demand from people wanting to live in the area, built on to provide low-rise homes and even shops, a school, sports hall, swimming baths, meeting centre or workshops. Introducing a mix of uses contravenes current zoning regulations, but would be sure to inject vibrant new activity into dead, abandoned areas.

Where renovation work is being carried out on an estate of several towers, one should be completed first to act as a 'show block'. The initial stage always generates tremendous enthusiasm, and residents in other blocks who may have been hesitant about joining a team can often be persuaded to think again. Signs of work in progress can also change the tone of the neighbourhood within days.

Build it yourself

Along with the self-help renovation projects, many people are now choosing to build their own homes from scratch. The self-build movement has grown increasingly in strength over the past decade and now, with some 14,000 homes of this kind being put up every year in England and Wales, has a higher output than large companies like Barratt or Wimpey. A recent acknowledgement of the movement and its successes was made early in 1989 when the Housing Corporation launched its Community Self-Build Agency. This is designed to encourage local authorities to take people from their housing lists and help them build their own homes.

Local councils could take a leaf out of Stirling District Council's book by making available reasonably priced housing plots on derelict land – ideal sites for people wanting to build their own homes. Simple financial packages can be devised where people from the council housing list are actually encouraged to find an ingenious way of jumping the queue. In Stirling, the local authority co-operated by allowing the sale of land at a reasonable rate and so provided the initial boost to trigger off the project. They were pragmatic enough to know that the land was basically worthless and did not hold on until some future date in the hope of achieving a higher price.

When a builder puts up a house he needs to ensure that he makes a profit. Usually small builders don't get large discounts from builder's merchants, but in Stirling the self-builders became the largest purchasers of building materials in the town for the period in which they worked. They didn't need to make a profit, so this element was not built into the calculations. They finished up having to pay only for building materials, the architect, the land and, where they did employ specialist builders, the individual sub-contractors. This saved £13,000 per house on property that would have cost £35,000 through traditional purchasing methods of buying a completed house from a builder.

Home improvements

The problems of decaying, privately owned homes in inner cities has to be tackled urgently. Many are in a poor state either because they are rented and neglected by the landlord, or because their owner-occupiers cannot afford to carry out renovation work. Much more encouragement is needed here from government, once again by improving the accessibility of grants instead of curtailing grant aid.

Any neglected housing, private or public sector, is open to abuse by vandals. If there is a serious intention to restore our cities, private home-owners also need help from central government to bring their properties up to a reasonable standard.

The only reason why such simplistic approaches have not been adopted is the complacency of central and local government and financiers. They have refused to acknowledge the findings of a plethora of reports and have not seen the wisdom in fostering an approach which starts with the basics – the provision of shelter – and then adopts a flexible approach to encourage ordinary people to break free from the rigid shackles imposed by a dependency regime.

Post-industrial packaging

The next stage in the regeneration of a typical British city is to look at new uses for huge derelict industrial buildings. So often they are still standing like bleak monoliths next to modern shopping centres and office blocks.

Companies could, for example, be offered attractive tax incentives to invest in certain schemes. Government could also offer to match spending on a ratio basis – if an investor is prepared to put up perhaps £4 million to reuse an old textile mill, then the state could offer a £1 million contribution. This system already exists on a piecemeal basis in the City Grant Schemes, but it could be widened to benefit more areas of development.

However, many of the poorest inner city sites require greater government funding – to encourage developers to build or regenerate the most problematical ones equal contributions would be more appropriate.

If the property happens to occupy a prime site there may be opportunities for planning gains to be made. Where developers are competing to restore a prime-site mill, an old railway station or a warehouse, the local authority can take advantage of the competition and suggest that the most attractive scheme, and therefore the one most likely to be given planning permission, would also involve the developer in building a nursery school, community hall, new roads or reasonably priced housing for the benefit of the local people. Preference should also be given to those schemes which employ local people.

Everyone involved should, in theory, reap rewards. Local people get jobs and extra facilities, the council profits because it secures extra social amenities at no cost to itself, and the granting of planning permission becomes a huge asset to developers because the site immediately increases in value.

Old industrial buildings have great advantages over almost anything that has followed because they are extremely well built, and offer flexibility for conversion – who would have thought fifty years ago that Battersea Power Station could ever have been thought of for a fun park? A redundant Victorian building, for example, could be turned into anything from an antiques market, gallery or shopping centre to small high-tech or crafts workshops, offices, flats or a leisure centre.

Again there is a need for planning changes to be made so that projects can incorporate a mixture of uses. Councils at the moment are reluctant to allow residential, retail and light industrial uses all in the same building. But I have proved that these ideas are feasible in the recent mill conversion scheme I have already described at Burnley in Lancashire.

I would suggest there is a huge demand in Britain now for between two and three million similar, flexible spaces. There are already encouraging signs that in post-industrial Britain we will see a resurgence of small family and one-person firms producing hand-crafted items. Many people, particularly the unemployed, have taken part in training courses only to find there are no job opportunities afterwards, and so self-employment is becoming increasingly popular.

During the Black Road scheme one resident, David Broadhead, who had been out of work for years, completed a joinery apprenticeship while restoring his house. He then used his new-found carpentry skills to set up a small business at home to restore furniture. Within two years he was running a thriving restoration business and in great demand in the town for producing quality products.

Other community projects have taught people skills in painting and decorating, electrics, plastering, masonry, bricklaying and accounting. In addition to those skills they also acquired enough self-confidence to reject state support through the dole and other social security benefits and set up their own businesses.

There is no reason why small companies could not provide, at a competitive rate, many items which are now frequently imported from abroad by the building industry – ceramic tiles, kitchen units, wrought iron spiral staircases, terracotta pots, machine-turned wood for door knobs and curtain rails, and so on. Around £3 billion worth of building materials are imported every year. The balance of trade figures would surely be given a useful boost if artisans were given more encouragement in Britain. Pride in self-achievement and a return to the ideas of William Morris with his flourishing arts and crafts movement could put Britain back on the map as a net exporter of quality building materials instead of having to import. These new artisan workshops could be located in and amongst the revitalized housing areas, where they should be.

I travel a lot throughout the world, either to give talks about my work or because of my political duties as president of the International Union of Architects. I see the hopelessness of political systems that stifle individual flair, such as those in the Eastern Bloc (excepting Hungary) where free enterprise is frowned on. In a way, the 1960s approach to housing in this country was not dissimilar. We, too, need a *perestroika* to free us from the inefficient bureaucracy which loses us so much human potential.

Shop horror

Shopping areas come next. Despite well-held views to the contrary, the remaining small, old streets in most cities have survived well, and usually need little more than a facelift. Here, very often, the old firms have sufficient guaranteed turnover to stay in business – though they are often run by non-white newcomers who are the only ones prepared to put in the long hours necessary to keep the business thriving. These areas are best left alone. The shopping boom of the mid-eighties has ensured prosperity in the high street, but unfortunately at a cost to the environment. The proliferation of, and competition between, chain stores has wrecked the character of shopping streets, and many shop frontages have been ruined with glass and aluminium. Huge eyesores including hypermarkets and DIY warehouses have also crept into city centres. The packaged, and often garish, image of each store often makes it difficult to distinguish one town from another.

Town planners could usefully be empowered to encourage more imaginative streetscapes. A few simple measures could be taken to avoid unsightly and brutal street frontages – by restricting the usage of illuminated neon signs, for example, and insisting on building with local materials. I would like to see the reintroduction of planning on a more local basis, which could function as the old bye-laws did and take account of the idiosyncrasies of villages and towns.

The worst retail catastrophes are the vast concrete shopping complexes of the sixties and seventies. Many of these are already largely shabby and dilapidated, and see a rapid turnover of traders. Others include the desolate general store on the huge residential estates.

The shopping complexes are far from being user-friendly, as I discovered when I took part in an experiment for the *Sunday Telegraph*. I was given a pram, two young children and a shopping list and set out for the Arndale Centre in Manchester. After struggling with the bus I then faced the dismal task of buying everything on my list. The first hurdle was negotiating the escalator from street level into the complex – it was virtually impossible with a pram and kids. And then came the shops – some wouldn't allow prams in, others had two-inch-high steps to cross and several, with sales space on two floors, left customers to walk up lengthy flights of stairs. The day was exhausting and depressing and not an experience I would choose to repeat: I'm sure that if there were more women architects, or more men who shopped with prams, these sorts of disasters would not happen.

Improving existing complexes is difficult, but once again I would propose that a mixture of uses, even with some offered at low rents, might ensure that empty premises do not simply fall victim to vandals. The shops could be augmented by workshops and offices, and the large, open walkways could make ideal market-places with stalls and local entertainers. Rain and wind are almost always a problem in precincts; the environment could be improved and bad weather kept out by roofing over the entire space. Local authorities have to be especially vigilant about the environmental upkeep of these places. More attention could be paid to land-scaping and ensuring that litter is not allowed to accumulate.

One of the main functions of a city or town is to act as a retail centre, so it is essential to keep shops in town centres. Out-of-town shopping complexes serve some purpose for people with cars who need to buy bulky items but if you take away the vitality of the central core it will be followed by a lack of public interest. People will vote with their feet, trade will diminish and set in train a cycle of decline leading to further decay and squalor. Shopping must be actively directed back to city and town centres.

Home office

Increasing use of computers is soon likely to introduce changes in the workplace. Within the next ten years the entire system could be transformed. Many people will be working from home linked by computer terminal to their headquarters. Visits to the office will become infrequent.

Such a change will have several beneficial effects – road and public transport systems will be under less strain particularly in the South-East, and fewer offices will be needed. Redundant office blocks unsuitable for conversion for use with computers, because the floor-to-ceiling heights leave insufficient space for installing the kind of floors required for mainframe computers, would be ideal for conversion to much-needed inner-city housing.

Suburbs

In the rest of my imaginary city the problems are fewer and less troublesome. The suburbs of most cities are not under stress. Homes are generally owner-occupied and well cared for, so all that is necessary is that these areas should continue to be well maintained. Setting aside spaces for heavy industry is one element of zoning which works – the largest, most disruptive factories are best kept outside town.

The work I have suggested in my plan to regenerate a city is not going to happen overnight. But by encouraging people to take the lead in improving housing I think that within the next few decades Britain could have resolved most of the damaging problems its towns and cities face today.

Country matters

Inner cities, however, do not have a monopoly on problems. Rural areas, too, have come under considerable threat. During the past twenty years many villages have undergone complete trans-formation. As more people become car owners there has been an invasion of new residents from nearby towns and cities, which has led in turn to the building of major new roads which have carved up the countryside.

Country living has become highly fashionable and the trend has put increasing pressure to expand on villages and small country towns: many now have their beautiful old centres ringed by modern, yuppie estates. The sprawl is eating up thousands of acres of unprotected farming land every year. Of course, if the cities were made more attractive places in which to live there would be a reduced threat to the green belt.

As villages have grown to provide more housing, they have also had to offer more extensive shopping facilities. As a result, particularly in the late seventies and early eighties, many local shops were extended or redeveloped into mini-markets or even supermarkets.

The influx of new cash has boosted property prices but put them out of reach of the local community. It is therefore all the more important to ensure that the indigenous population has a good income, but with changes such as increased mechanization and over-production on farms the countryside has seen a decline in jobs and a migration by the younger generation to the towns and cities. Left in the wake are numerous farm buildings which have been allowed to fall into decay. Countless large houses and churches are also desperately in need of repair.

The loss of a capable workforce is highly damaging, and to keep villages alive a regeneration of the rural areas is essential. Unemployed farm workers already possess practical skills, and so building renovation could be introduced as a new industry. In the same way that the National Urban Renewal Agency proposals could work for cities, a similar funding body could be set up in rural areas to redevelop farms, generate jobs for skilled craftsmen, restore heritage sites and increase tourism. Schemes for building low-cost housing to enable young people to marry and raise families in the areas in which they were brought up need all the encouragement they can get. At Longnor in the Peak District, for instance, a local housing association has built very acceptable traditional homes in keeping with the village vernacular. These are available for local people at subsidized rents. Only with a continuing pool of this kind of housing, and some kind of revitalization of the rural economy, will genuine country communities in many parts of Britain continue to exist into the twenty-first century.

Prince Charles' Dorchester expansion is awaited with keen anticipation. Will this set a new trend in high-quality vitalization of rural areas?

A new beginning

As for the architects, they have a chance to rehabilitate their professional role and win back much-needed friends from amongst the public at large. Frequently at the bottom of the appreciation stakes, their popularity will greatly improve if they once again restore their nerve and take up the challenges before them. Retreating behind the Modernist drawing board is not enough; active promotion of their skills and visions for the benefit of the community is essential. All architects could be community architects. The demand is there, let them meet the challenge.

Although this book marks the end of an era, it also signals the beginning of another. With the proliferation of studies and reports, we are witnessing increased public awareness of the many and varied problems facing our environment and should all have learned a great deal. The trend towards green politics, conservation, restoration and a more humanitarian attitude must be warmly applauded. Government, architects, planners and financiers should all adopt a new approach. They should be willing to serve rather than dictate. It is no longer up to the state to sort out problems – the future lies in our own hands.

Bibliography

ALLAUN, F. *No Place Like Home – Britain's Housing Tragedy*, Andre Deutsch, London, 1972

ARCHBISHOP OF CANTERBURY'S COMMISSION ON URBAN PRIORITY AREAS, *Faith in the City: A Call for Action by Church and Nation*, Church House Publishing, London, 1985

ARTLEY, Alexandra, and ROBINSON, John Martin. *The New Georgian Handbook: A First Look at the Conservation Way of Life*, Ebury Press, London, 1985

BANHAM, Reyner. *The Architecture of the Well-tempered Environment*, Architectural Press/University of Chicago Press, London/Chicago, 1969

BELL, Colin and Rose. *City Fathers: The Early History of Town Planning in Britain*, Pelican/Penguin, Harmondsworth, 1972. First published by Barrie & Rockliff, The Cresset Press, 1967

BINNEY, Marcus. *Our Vanishing Heritage*, Arlington Books, London, 1984

BLAKE, Peter. *Form Follows Fiasco: Why Modern Architecture Hasn't Worked*, Atlantic/Little, Brown, Boston and Toronto, 1977

BRANDT, W. *North-South: A Programme for Survival*, Pan, London, 1980

BROADBENT, G., BUNT, R., JENCKS, C. *Signs, Symbols and Architecture*, J. Wiley, England, 1980

BUCKMINSTER FULLER, R. *Utopia or Oblivion: the Prospects for Humanity*, Allen Lane, Penguin Books, Harmondsworth, 1970

CANTACUZINO, Sherban, and BRANDT, Susan. *Saving Old Buildings*, Architectural Press, London, 1980

CHARLES, HRH THE PRINCE OF WALES. *A Vision of Britain*, Doubleday, London, 1989

COLEMAN, Alice. *Utopia on Trial: Vision and Reality in Planned Housing,* Hilary Shipman, London, 1985

CORBUSIER, Le. *Towards a New Architecture,* Architectural Press, London, 1946

DAVIS, Barbara (Ed.) *Remaking Cities,* Proceedings of the 1988 International Conference in Pittsburgh, University of Pittsburgh Press, Pittsburgh, 1989

DUNLEAVY, Patrick. *The Politics of Mass Housing in Britain, 1945–1975,* Clarendon Press, Oxford, 1981. Published in the USA by Oxford University Press, New York

FITZWALTER, Raymond and TAYLOR, David. *Web of Corruption: The Story of John Poulson and T. Dan Smith,* Granada Publishing Limited, St Albans, Herts, 1981

GIBSON, Tony, et al. *Us Plus Them: How to Use the Experts to Get What People Really Want,* Town and County Planning Association, London, 1986

HALL, P. *Cities of Tomorrow,* Blackwell, 1988

HARRISON, Paul. *Inside the Inner City: Life under the Cutting Edge,* Penguin Books, London and Harmondsworth, 1981

H.M. GOVERNMENT. *Policy for the Inner Cities* HMSO, London, 1977

HUGHES, Robert. *The Shock of the New,* BBC, London, 1980

HUTCHINSON, Maxwell. *The Prince of Wales. Right or Wrong?* Faber, London, 1989

JENCKS, Charles. *Le Corbusier and the Tragic View of Architecture,* Harvard University Press, Cambridge, Massachusetts, USA, 1973

JENCKS, Charles. *The Prince, The Architects and New Wave Monarchy,* Academy Editions, London, 1988

KNEVITT, Charles. *Space on Earth, Architecture: People and Buildings,* Thames Television International Ltd., London, 1985

KNEVITT, Charles and WATES, Nick. *Community Architecture: How people can shape their own environment,* Penguin, Harmondsworth, 1986

KRIER, R. *Urban Space,* Academy Editions, London, 1979

LASDUN, Denys (Ed.) *Architecture in an Age of Scepticism*, Heinemann, London, 1984

LENNARD, S.H.C. and H.L. *Livable Cities*, The Centre for Urban Well-Being, Gondolier Press, New York, 1987

LOWENTHAL, David and BINNEY, Marcus (Eds.) *Our Past Before Us: Why Do We Save It?* Temple Smith, London, 1981

MORRIS, D. and HESS, K. *Neighbourhood Power: The new Localism*, Beacon, London, 1975

NEWMAN, Oscar. *Defensible Space: Crime Prevention through Urban Design*, Macmillan, New York, 1972

NEWMAN, O. *Defensible Space: People and Design in the Violent City*, Architectural Press, London, 1972

PAWLEY, Martin. *Architecture versus Housing*, Studio Vista, London, 1971. Published in the USA by Praeger Publishers, New York and Washington

POSOKHIN, M.V. *Cities to Live In*, Novosti Press Agency Publishing House, Moscow, 1974

REPORT OF THE INDEPENDENT INQUIRY INTO DISTURBANCES OF OCTOBER, 1985 THE BROADWATER FARM ESTATE, TOTTENHAM. *The Broadwater Farm Inquiry*, Karia Press, London, 1986

REPORT OF THE INDEPENDENT INQUIRY INTO THE DISTURBANCES OF OCTOBER 1985, Tottenham. (Second Report) *Broadwater Farm Revisited*, Karia Press, London, 1989

ROCK, David. *The Grass Roots Developers: A Handbook for Town Development Trusts*, RIBA, London, 1980

ROGERS, Richard. *Richard Rogers & Architects*, Academy Editions/St Martin's Press, London, 1985

ROYAL INSTITUTE OF BRITISH ARCHITECTS. *A National Urban Renewal Agency*, RIBA London, 1987

ROYAL INSTITUTE OF BRITISH ARCHITECTS. *Highfield Hall: A Community Project*, RIBA, London, 1983

ROYAL INSTITUTE OF BRITISH ARCHITECTS. *Tenants participation in housing design: a guide for action*, 1988

RUDOFSKY, B. *Architecture without Architects*, Doubleday & Co.,

New York, 1964/Academy Editions, London, 1977, 1981

SCARMAN, The Rt Hon. Lord. *The Brixton Disorders, 10–12 April, 1981*, (The Scarman Report) HMSO, London, 1981. Penguin Books, London and Harmondsworth, 1982

SCHUMACHER, E.F. *Small is Beautiful: A Study of Economics as if People Mattered*, Abacus/Sphere Books, London, 1974. First published by Blond & Briggs, London, 1973

SCOTT, Geoff. *Building Disasters and Failures*, The Construction Press, Lancaster, 1976

SEELIG, M.Y. *The Architecture of Self Help Communities*, Architectural Record Books, New York, 1978

SERRANO, Jose Luis Ospina. *Housing Ourselves: Popular Participation in Housing in Columbia and England*, University of York, Institute of Advanced Architectural Studies, York, 1985

SMITH, Jenny. *Urban Renewal: Securing Community Involvement*. Community Projects Foundations, London, 1983

SNEDDON, Jim and THEOBALD, Caroline (Eds.). *Building Communities*, Community Architecture Information Services in association with RIBA Publications, London, 1987

TAYLOR, Nicholas. *The Village in the City*, Published in association with New Society, Temple Smith, London, 1973

TERRY, Quinlan. *Quinlan Terry*, Architectural Design/Academy Editions, London, 1981

TEYMUR, N., MARKUS, T. and WOOLLEY, T. (Eds.) *Rehumanising Housing*, Butterworths, 1983

TOMKINSON, Martin and GILLARD, Michael. *Nothing to Declare: The Political Corruptions of John Poulson*, John Calder (Publishers) Ltd, 1980

WARD, Colin. *Tenants Take Over*, Architectural Press, London, 1974

WARD, Colin. *Housing: an anarchist approach*, Freedom Press, London, 1976

WARD, Colin. *The Child in the City*, Penguin Books, Harmondsworth, 1979

WARD, Colin. *When We Build Again: Let's Have Housing That Works!*, Pluto Press, London, 1985

WARD, Colin. *Welcome, Thinner City*, Bedford Square Press, September 1989

WILSON, Des. with ANDREWS, Leighton and FRANLEZ, Maurice. *Citizen Action: Taking Action in your Community*, Longman, London, 1986

WOLFE, Tom. *From Banhaus to Our House*, Jonathan Cape, London, 1982

WOOLLEY, Thomas Adrian. *Community Architecture: an evaluation of the case for user participation in architectural design*, Thesis, May 1985.

Index

Italic numerals refer to illustration numbers.

Index

Index

Index